SEARCHING FOR SENSE

TO THE ST. PHILIP NERI PARISH FAMILY
THE CHILDREN, TEEN-AGERS,
YOUNG ADULTS, MIDDLE-AGED, AND AGED
WHO
IN THEIR BIRTHS, LIVES, PAINS,
AND EVEN DEATHS,
HAVE TAUGHT ME
MORE DEEPLY
THE GENIUS OF CATHOLICISM
THIS BOOK IS DEDICATED

The
Logic of
Catholic
Belief

Searching For Sense

Frank
De Siano
of the Paulist Fathers

Cover Design: Dan Pezza

NIHIL OBSTAT:
Rev. Msgr. Edmund G. Van Der Zanden
Censor Deputatus

IMPRIMATUR:
✠ Most Reverend Cornelius M. Power, D.D., J.C.D.
Archbishop of Portland
May 23, 1975

Library of Congress
Catalog Card Number: 75-23155

ISBN: 0-8091-1886-6

Published by Paulist Press
Editorial Office: 1865 Broadway, N.Y., N.Y. 10023
Business Office: 400 Sette Drive, Paramus, N.J. 07652

Printed and bound in the
United States of America

CONTENTS

Acknowledgments

I would like to thank the Paulist Fathers whose education, support, and friendship have given me far more than I could ever repay.

Next, my thanks goes to John Kirvan who saw a little article of mine in the *Homiletic and Pastoral Review* and twisted my arm into turning the ideas into this book.

Also, I cannot thank enough the people of St. Philip Neri Parish in Portland, Oregon, to whom I dedicate this book. Their support and kindness to me as I began my ministry is a priceless thing. I only ask their forgiveness if working on this book has taken me from things I should have been doing with them.

Dr. John Beaulieu has been more than a friend to me; he was a patient sounding board, a diligent pursuer, helping me with the rough drafts of this book. He has my deep thanks.

Finally, I should mention that the excerpts from Scripture have been taken, more or less, from the New American Bible.

Introduction

How can anyone be a Catholic? It causes both amazement and skepticism. Catholics are superstitious, elitist, self-satisfied, anti-scientific, anti-common sense. Their faith has been picked apart from without and within—especially within. All those smooth syllogisms of only fifteen years ago have died at the hands of Catholic thinkers; the elaborate liturgical drama of the Mass has been stripped. Once secure and obvious, now the grand old faith has taken on insecurity; the perception of the world—at last—has shown what an irrelevant set of propositions the Catholic faith truly is.

So many sit before us to judge us. They have things figured out a bit. And a bit seems enough. There is no difficulty with God—they like that idea. But a Church is something else. They are independent, philosophically cool, poised, pioneers, taking their own measurement of God and faith, buying some, rejecting some, but basically standing alone. I have even heard it put in terms of Plato—the ideal always escapes us, so why get involved in a Church when no Church will do.

Life means searching, putting down feet for only a second or two, moving from city to city, from value to value, from group to group. So there is no reason to get hung up, especially to get hung up on something like the Catholic faith. Of all the crosses to be placed on someone's back, Catholicism seems the greatest. Go

1

West, young man, or East or anywhere, but don't get caught.

So there I sit, a priest, judged by my peers, the collared-shirt read as a striped prison uniform, imprisoned by a vision shattered and cracked, by blinkers that prevent a nod to the right or the left.

Yet I know what searching means. I have done a bit of it myself—searching my own heart to know what God is asking, searching the faces of men to find what they are asking, searching down a thousand turns of Christian thought, searching for a peace that rests the heart, searching for a vision that makes some sense. So I am not much different from anyone else. We all are searchers.

In fact, that is precisely why I am a Catholic. Part of what it means to be a searcher lies in daring to ask not trivial or simple, but complex and profound questions. Questions about the meaning of man, the destiny of the world, the kind of God we affirm, what we can ultimately expect. But you are not a serious searcher if anything will do. To be satisfied with any answer is to play games with questions. If you insist life is playing games and posing questions, these games and questions are for real.

Deep inside, we know that. And that is why we dabble. We so much fear the greatness of reality, the utter mystery in our minds, the suspected grandeur of our lives, that we push our questions into cocktail-talk, little sprinklings of would-be insights, all the while ramming ourselves through vast amounts of work so we can forget even what the point of working is.

That's why the Church makes sense. It keeps the questions from slipping. It keeps the tension alive. It gives enough of an answer to form a diving board, to make a hook to hang life on, to give us the gall to raise up our heads in an otherwise brutal universe.

What I am asking for is a chance—a chance to say what being a Catholic means, how being a Catholic brings meaning to life, how the Catholic ties enough together to make his way in life. You will find no "proof" in here—one never proves love. But you will find some plausibility, plausibility to make the Catholic faith at least temptable.

My argument is very simple. There are only a few options to take in life, a few decisions about God and man. If one can accept a God who is mighty and who can care for us at the same time; if one can see that people need people; if one can resist the cynical cop-out of dismissing man as worthless, as a tragic jest—then the yarn of the Catholic Church is in one's hands already. You merely have to knit a little, and the whole genius of Catholicism starts to form.

We rightly prize our independence and the achievements we've accomplished in life. Independence and achievement mark the nature of man as deeply as anything else. But independence need not mean solitude, and achievement has a way of slipping by into memory or dream. Man, for all his greatness, *is* like the grass which fades, as a psalmist might put it. Religion arises as God renewing the greatness of man—as God taking man seriously enough to transform him.

For every ounce of self-belief, there is an equal ounce of doubt. Strangely, God believes in us more than we believe in ourselves. Catholicism ultimately means a double creed, a creed of man's belief in God, and God's belief in us. And only when we reach this level can we assess ourselves as we really are, can we get down to the real business of seeking and finding, of playing the game of life for keeps.

My plea is that we get beyond the "images" of Catholicism to the real meat of Catholic sense. It is too easy to get lost in clouds of incense, Hollywood-styled excommunications, sentimental statues, necks bedecked with medals. My plea is that someone who believes enough in God and man to even raise the issue will find in Catholic life the image of Christ, the God who takes our flesh. My plea, in short, is that we read our hearts carefully enough to know the dilemmas and what kind of solution they demand.

This book is simple. Within its simple strokes there may be some subtle gestures, some complicated plays. Life is like that—the simple images we have of ourselves belie the complex twists of human living. Take any piece of life and pull at it—sure enough, a thread comes loose which leads to other threads, which leads to everything. Man is wrapped in mystery. But moving from the simple to the complex, from the face to the personality, and moving back from the complex to the simple, from the many layers to the outer layer, brings us to an appreciation of ourselves and the God who made us and saves us.

At any rate, nothing is lost. At the very least, you may be more convinced that being a Catholic is a ridiculous act. But at the very most, you may be convinced that the sense of Catholicism is the sense of God and man, the sense you've been trying to make and trying to find ever since you started to search.

At the very least, it's worth a try.

1 God

The sweat of a Washington summer appears without any effort; breathing in the nation's capital is enough to tax the ability of any anti-perspirant. I swung the laundry bag over my back and entered the laundromat, dozens of soapy machines bleaching steam in a steamy city.

Then it happened. A fine looking black woman spotted first my white face, and then my black collar; she could not suppress her enthusiasm. "Glory, brother, are you a believer?" I quickly surveyed the room to see if anyone else was keeping track of this spiritual accosting. Nothing like this had ever happened to me before. A few were looking, some smiling, but the grinding and gurgling of washing machines afforded a bit of privacy.

"Well, yes, I am," I answered with some hesitation. It seemed to me a situation of reverse blasphemy: one doesn't think of sex in a church, nor does one think of God in a laundromat. Besides, I thought my black shirt would be an obvious answer to her question.

But she pursued. "Well, so am I. The Lord is just wonderful, isn't he, brother?" I had to admit he was. I kind of liked the Lord.

"Has he ever spoken to you?" she continued. I paused to get her meaning. My mind flashed back to hours of sleepy meditations, moments of stillness in a darkened chapel, times when prayer was extended, begging, reaching for God, pleading with him, arguing, accepting. There were words—mine. Things were screwy, not fitting in; I needed his help, I needed *him*. But no words came back—rather, only wordless peace, assurance, a hidden hand clasping a raw spirit.

Yes, I supposed he had talked to me. But was this what she was looking for? Did she see the Lord in white robes and smiling face, giving instructions on how to live, or answers to particular questions? Is this what she wanted?

"I suppose he has talked to me," was my ventured answer. "Well," she closed in, "if he had, you'd know it. He talked to me and it was beautiful." I leaned over the washer to put in soap, half hiding from her intensity, half fearing she would expose me as the worst of believers—one who affirms with shreds of doubt, without irrefutable evidence.

"Brother, it's so good to know we have believers in the world. It's so good to have a few who know the Lord." I wasn't sure whether she was including me or not, and I did not care too much for her judging, separating sheep and goats, believers and non-believers. But I looked up and smiled. "God has a way of getting to us all," I responded, but with a tone of voice that indicated our conversation should end, that I should be let off her hook. We assured each other of our prayers and parted, each to our own machines.

At the first possible moment, I got outside and around the corner to enjoy a cigarette.

God has a way of getting to us all.

*

God has become for most of us some kind of embarrassment. Our desire instinctively is to keep God shelved and contained: in some corner of our private life, perhaps, or even in a building where he can sooth distraught people who need him. We want him around; most of us have no grudges against him. But we want him on our terms, subject to our conditions, doing only so much and no more.

We certainly don't want him intruding into our controlled world. While once God explained all things ordinary and extraordinary, we now expect him to explain very little. He can hold all things in existence if he wants to. But we will manage everything else. After all, we mustn't be gullible.

The containment of God began in modern thought with some drastic blows against accepted theological doctrine. The Bible seemed to say that the sun goes around the earth. But it doesn't. Strike one! The doctrine of evolution nibbled away at the simple and majestic view of creation—God creating the world as it is by means of his direct word, or God making things like children playing in the mud. Strike two! And all those demons fleeing and shrieking from Jesus' gaze today seem more likely to be overly suppressed id's or epileptic fits. Strike three!

So we get embarrassed. Instead of having God working everywhere, we prefer him to work nowhere. And we do this for his protection as much as for our own protection. We do not want him cornered, proved not to be where we thought he was. Nor do we want our hard-won theories challenged and confused by interventions, and miracles, and things of that sort.

Actually, though, the containment of God has a long history. Jewish thinkers always saw God as acting quite differently from humans: "My thoughts are not your thoughts, nor are my ways your ways, says the

Lord" (Is. 55:9). This grew to rather refined heights in Jewish revelation. When the Jewish state collapsed and the cream of the Jewish nation was captured in Babylon, the Jews learned well that God could not be counted on in any automatic sense. Where previously it was thought that anyone who kept God's law was guaranteed success and prosperity, now such simple ideas were strewn among the ashes of Jerusalem. God was much subtler than people thought. In later Jewish thought, God was shielded from the created world by echelons of angels who acted for him. Involved, but only so much, God became graciously distant.

This distance was magnified and intensified when Jewish thought mingled with Greek ideas of God's perfection and unknowability. God was so infinite, so unchanging, so real that he was virtually unknowable. What could such a God possibly have to do with us? How could measly minds like ours approach him or grasp him? Humans were not embarrassed with God; they were only giving God his due.

The paradox in this derives from our utter need for revelation (after all, we could not know God so he would have to make himself known) and the extreme difficulty of receiving revelation. If God is so different from us, how does he make himself known, how *can* he make himself known? What words will he give us? What songs would be adequate? So we are forced to play with God—keeping him near and far, unknown and yet revealed.

Of course, back then, people saw the world as evil —wars, sickness, early death, natural setbacks, all the products of scientific ignorance. Today the world is much more pleasant. We can manage things enough to make life enjoyable, and when life is not, various pills and treatments help us cope. But whether the world is evil (and we keep God away to maintain his purity) or good (and we keep God away because we have no need for him), we have found ways to contain him.

Our own slant on containing God comes from the age of mechanization, in which the universe is conceived in terms of forces and counter-forces which make sense out of things. Where once Christians simply viewed God as holding all in order, giving structure to the marvelous world in which they lived, the great physicists Galileo and Newton, and their followers in the next centuries, showed that much of the world was explainable on its own. The order of the world was latent in the world. We had no need for God to provide order at every moment; if he provided it once, then that would be enough to keep the world going. Enchanted by the prospect of obvious explanation, culture proceeded to banish God from every sector. "Deism" emerged: it said that God wound up the world like a watch, and now it ticked on its own.

And we are children of the age of mechanization. Our machines work far more efficiently than those of the eighteenth century. God is terribly transcendent for us. We have no need to look for his interventions; when we pray for God's aid, we do so with doubt. Like children who have left home and lost contact with their parents, we have found it necessary to make God distant, and we cringe that he may get in touch with us again. What would we say? How would we handle it?

Far better to have God, but have him aloof. Give God his due, we think; make God transcendent and keep him from our world. So we hone our syllogisms and formulate our position carefully: if God is God, he cannot be a cause alongside other causes; for if God were to act directly in our world, he would become a cause alongside other causes, losing his transcendence, and thus he would not be God. So for God's very protection, we insulate him from our world, wrap him up in church or private prayer, safe from scholars, scientists, artists, politicians, and sometimes even churchmen.

Yet here we sit, talking about God, thinking about prayer, wondering about salvation, touched by enough passion for God that we know getting rid of him would be absurd, ceasing to question him a tragedy. Talk about being, or ground of being, or self-transcending being, or one, or all, or whatever—we are still talking of the center of reality and the center of our own selves. God is too crucial to us for to place him on the side.

For God makes a difference. He makes a difference in that a banished God leaves us terribly alone, leaves us at the mercy of our own constructs—and our constructs have as many qualities of terror as they have of beauty. He makes a difference in our joy, for he can give a reality to it which we cannot; he makes a difference in our despair, for that temptation grows with our increasing solitude.

So what do we do? Shelve God in pristine purity and rob the core of our religious hearts? Or do we fold God into the covers of our lives to such an extent that he becomes an idol among other idols, the ready answer to flippant questions, the band-aid of human frivolity?

God's transcendence has made simply too much sense to abandon it. Too often God has been identified with finite things, with particular cultures, with ambiguous and distorted images. God's transcendence has been the best insurance against this. How, after all, can God be trapped and enclosed in limited, particular events and things? Idolatry, so wisely proscribed in the first commandment, grows with its steady malignancy when God's transcendence is abandoned. Constricted to one place and time, he is thereby elbowed out of other space and time. In short, God becomes provincial.

Yet the sense we find in affirming God's transcendence does not mean that God must be contained, protected from our world. Rather, in affirming God's transcendence, we are only trying to say that God is Lord.

God is Lord of all there is, freely giving existence to all there is, generously caring for everything. His transcendence does not mean his absence from creation; rather, his transcendence means his free action throughout *all* of creation. Instead of being protected from all human and worldly events, God is Lord over all human and worldly events. Unable to be limited and captured, he freely gives and bestows, freely starts and starts again, freely loves and gives himself.

God's transcendence means that he is open to every moment, working in and through every moment with the full, compact, unlimited resources of his very being. It means he is always present. It means there is no difference between the ordinary and extraordinary. It means he lets our freedom and history unfold as it will; it means he works in and through our freedom and history to bring about his will.

Saying God is Lord does not tie him down to our moments and our limitations; it frees us to understand God as dealing with our moments and limitations. Saying God is Lord does not make him a cause alongside other causes, the one who merely provides the metal and the know-how while we apply these elements in the factory and distribute them through stores so we can get a can opener to open a can. Instead, God is cause of all causes, free over all causes, free to call, free to move, free to love. As the being of all beings, God is free over all beings. As timeless Lord, he can enter all times.

We find God an embarrassment when we compete with him, wanting to be God ourselves, juxtaposing him against ourselves to make us the underdog winners by default. Let's face it: we love to whimper. We love to pout, to rage against authority. When we are sober, though, reflecting in the quiet of our rooms and the silence of our souls, we know God will not let us play with him like that. He's too far above us, he's far too close to us.

No one wants to make God manipulable by human whim and caprice. No one wants him stripped and exposed. We only want God to be seen in such a way that he can be God, placing himself in our hands, presenting himself to our searching, giving himself to our hearts.

If we fully recognize God as Lord, then we've insured him against manipulation. If God is Lord, we cannot demand that he act as we wish, nor presume he is working where we want him to, nor assume his grace whenever we need it. Too many have made fools of themselves and of God by cornering him, yelling "miracle" or "we are chosen" or some other slogan which amounts to religious insult. God's transcendence means that we cannot predict him, outguess him, or sidestep him. God's lordship shows that God is the actor, the doer, the revealer, the one who graces, and we have only the privilege of listening and watching, careful not to miss a move.

What is the sense of Catholicism about God? Just the basic sense that men have always made of him, pruned from distortions that contradict religion (like treating God as if he weren't God, or containing God to keep him from us). The object of religion is to bring God and man together; there is no other response to the pricking of our consciousness and anxiety of our souls but to bring God and man together, creator and creature, lover and beloved, savior and saved.

This sense of God means that God is not totally ungraspable by us. He is near. He can act. He can show himself to us. While we are radically different from God, he has made us also radically similar to him—able to search for him, even able to find him. God can consort with us, speak to us, make himself known. Though we can never exhaust him by our words or actions, he can get hold of enough of us to make a difference in our lives. This means that God can come—close in our hearts, quickly in our minds, surprisingly in our lives, stunningly in his Son.

There is no need to wince in laundromats, to blush when God is mentioned, to attribute to him our short-sightedness, to blame him for our faults. We only have to measure honestly the needs of our hearts and assess fairly the God of our hope.

2 Man

People. We need them. And we don't.

There are times when I'm ready to climb the walls. Things are quiet, slow. Nothing is going on. Seconds crawl like hours. My mind slips again and again from the desk: the ideas won't come, the words won't form, the background music is anxiously disturbing.

Discipline, I tell myself. Stick with it. You're doing something important, or at least necessary. Keep grinding away. Forget the boredom; stifle the loneliness.

But the words keep crowding together, the pages blur, the mind dangles in between four ideas that seem like no idea. I keep drawing a blank.

So I go looking, searching for someone who can take my mind off things, give me a bit of companionship, provide a few moments of humor or diversion, offer the right metaphor without knowing the subject, or show me that the desk is not the universe and life is broader than the task at hand.

I go searching to get in touch. Maybe a walk, maybe just a chat, but with someone else who has his concerns, his viewpoint, his own version of life. Someone who can touch my life with a bit of variety, who can play another tune when the record of my mind keeps skipping.

Surprisingly, someone is always there. We are not fussy in these situations. We need someone, we need anyone. When the world gets to be too much, it's our world getting to be too much. Yes, I'll take another world; yes, I'd be happy to step behind another's eyes. The pause that refreshes.

It's so hard to pause. Desk work, mechanical work, business, studies, planning, preventing, deciding: loneliness creeps in by way of many crevices. The world opens up in a yawn large enough to swallow every shred of energy. So we all go running—we've all got to get away, to find another, so we can find ourselves.

Even the most independent of us—and I'm an independent sort—just cannot cut it alone. The plug comes loose and our insides drip away, quickly or slowly, and soon we are empty. We can take pressure, quiet, noise, criticism, and a crowded schedule. But we cannot take being alone. Work itself is not the problem; work that closes us off, there's the problem. Work that forces us inside a narrow world, that makes us plod along without relief, soon forces the valves to pop as our feet go scrambling: anywhere, anyone, but not here, by myself.

People. We need them. Until we're trying to get home and the traffic won't move, and the temperature is burning us up, and we've worked so hard we're not even sure we want to eat, and rows of humans creep ahead of us, some cutting in, some not moving at all, and we discover the problem is a solitary flat tire that has kept thousands of people waiting half an hour or so, fuming and stewing, cursing this blessed life we're made for ourselves. Then we don't need people quite so much. In fact, we hate the sight of them.

How many times has the telephone rung for just

one time too many? One more person asking a silly question, complaining, coming up with more work for us to do. We hold our temper. control the tone of voice, and promise ourselves we'll yank the jack from the wall as soon as the party has hung up.

We've perhaps moved away from the city. A nice quiet street. Lawns mowed and green. Houses painted and cars washed. We've put up with city life, with fear and insult, just too long. So we move to the suburbs and sit on our porches marveling at how fresh the air seems. Our yards are fenced. Our mortgage is being paid off. This is "ours"—the well-earned castle.

Then one evening, perhaps at PTA, a guest speaker starts to take it all apart. It seems our fine neighborhood, our nice streets and lovely homes, are the perfect target for some "elements" who are making a killing by selling drugs. Not to someone else. But to our own children. Dear little Mary. Friendly John. Saving up their allowances or stealing things from here and there (remember the rumors we heard and suppressed) so they could buy a joint, or maybe something worse.

And no one keeps his dog fenced in. And no one keeps his kid off my yard. And no one taught Freddy how to drive well enough so he bumped into the car. And shopping centers and drive-ins have turned our nice street into a super highway. And those people so-and-so sold their house to: grass not cut, roaches probably in the kitchen. And little Johnny drinks while he puffs his joints.

So where do we go now? Out to the farm? Shall we move farther and farther away from the hell of civilization, away from our reputed racial enemies, away from crime, drugs, drink? Or does it all follow us there, too, even on the farm, the decay of society eating away, cancer in even the healthiest body?

All those fine things advertised and displayed in the women's magazines become uncanny jokes, projected relics of the unfilfilled utopia. We want to construct a fine society; we discover instead that our problems always follow us. We attempt to insulate ourselves from people, but people are always there. We seek the good life, but end up wondering if life is good at all.

People. We want to escape from them—sometimes even at a party, when the fifth person turns around and smiles at us, "Have you seen any good movies lately?" We want to escape—and scream.

*

So we have infatuation and disinfatuation with our fellow-man. We dally in between, seeking the touch of our fellow-man, fleeing his grasp. We concoct images of the perfect society, but then we view ourselves riding off alone in the sunset, pioneers in our own universe.

How much are we a part of each other? Are we programmed for others, needing them as much as we need anything? Or are we meant to be alone, tolerating others until we're brave enough to fly from our nests?

Put in these terms, the answer is simple. Whether we call it "city," or "community," or "fellowship," the ultimate truth is that we need each other. *Man is social.* Try any combination of ideas, any experiment of life, man has to stand with man.

We can let our imaginations play for a moment. Suppose we envision those "first particles" of existence, floating in unconsciousness, acknowledging a bi-focal thrust toward nothingness and toward God. Nothingness brings fear, but God induces them to survive. Instinctively, they cringe, they come together, magnetized by the strangeness of being at all, the weirdness of dancing in a vacuum. They come together to atoms, to molecules, to gasses and dust, to nebulae and galaxies, to stars and planets, to mountain and man.

From our suspicious glances to our modest handshakes, from intense reproduction to extensive organization, man mirrors the ingrained strangeness and wonder of existing; he reflects the need not to stand alone. Beneath it all, aloneness must surrender to extinction.

Take away society and you've taken it all away. Sever atom from atom, sever man from man, all that's left is nonsense, chaos, primeval terror.

Society is fundamental to every achievement man has made. For what do we have if we strip away what community has given us? Entertainment? Commerce? Family? Love? Language? Thought? We have, in fact, nothing—nothing but the unconscious tension of existence, tense to merge once again. Like a turntable that keeps rejecting on itself, life would keep returning together. The pattern of togetherness is simply too essential.

The need for socialization produces the very fabric of our human life. We all have had dreams, profound dreams, woven from strands of our life, but our dreams become realities only by cooperating with others. Some of us have had breakthroughs, but breakthroughs mean nothing unless others recognize them, feel them. If we have something to say, we don't say it to ourselves; rather, we say it to others.

Farming, domestication, the tribal hunt, the small village, the thriving port, the international city; the groping gesture, the primitive grunts, the early arguments, the fruitful dialogue, the profound discourse, the simple smile, the drive to endure, the elaborate courtship, the wonder of love: all these pieces form a mosaic, each pre-shaped for the finished image of man needing man, of man living with man.

Here is the reason why we hate to be alone. Here is the reason for our cities, our culture. As the human brain bunches together all the nerves of the human, so social man forms communities which bunch together the diversity and individuality of persons.

As much as we sometimes want to be alone, we can only do this because of contact we have had with others. The visions of living in the desert, in peaceful solitude, form in our heads because we have learned to think and act for ourselves; we have learned that surviving is worthwhile. But we learn that from others.

The frustrations we feel with society parallels the frustration we feel with the human body. Bodies, human and social, have long been blamed for many ills. Whereas the human body once was scorned as lustful and deceptive, now, with the human body glorified, we vent our frustrations on the social body, corrupt and deceptive. But we get nowhere without both bodies. To take the social nature of man seriously shows the same common sense of taking the physical nature of man seriously.

Society's sickness does not demonstrate the need for society's termination. It shows, rather, the need for society's salvation.

*

Behind the infatuation and dis-infatuation we feel about others lies the infatuation and dis-infatuation we feel about ourselves. We seem so important and like-wise so utterly ridiculous. Hours of every day are spent on ourselves: those neat new razor blades that pamper my face after it has been squished in lemon-smelling cream, my hair, my nails, my teeth (are they white enough?), my shower, powder between my toes, my sacred cup of morning coffee, my meals prepared as I like them, my conversations rigged to show my wis-dom, even my sloppy clothes arranged to make an im-pression. How important I am! How could the world get along without me?

How hard I have to work to keep myself likable—as if it all were to crumble once the truth got out. The truth about myself. My real smallness. My hidden thoughts which I fear others can read. Those terribly base motives behind my noble gestures. My greed. My lust. My feelings of not being at home with myself. My desire to flee from God.

If I doubt the worth of being with others, I also doubt the worth of being. Frankly, I am tempted to cynicism. Like all of us.

Cynicism is idealism gone sour, and we have had a close enough look at ourselves by the time we are twenty to make many ideals go sour. Here is man, the noblest of animals; but really he is just an animal with "nobility" as a questionable modifier. Here is man, the generous seeker of good; but he really seeks his own good, if he can even find that, with selfish calculation . Scratch deeply enough and you find the pus.

The question is: Where shall we place man's illu-sions? Is it that he overestimates himself, thinking that his life is significant when he should really adjust him-self to the more realistic view that he is an "accident" (a freak!) of nature? Or is it that he underestimates the sickness of his spirit, overlooking the disease of his soul, the lust behind every wish, the smallness behind every reach, the murder behind every handshake?

It's amazing—our capacity to tear to shreds and dismember the rational animal some say we are, to doubt the possibility of any real goodness in the human heart, to doubt our worth. Whether from our observant minds or our doctrines of corruption, it amounts to the same thing: we are cynical about ourselves—and yet we do not want to be.

Really, though, what will cynicism yield except defeat? Certainly, it provides no solution. Cynicism basically undercuts every bit of worth in the human project, leaving no alternative except extinction. I can be cynical and say "Everything is only atoms," or I can be cynical religiously by saying "Man is innately corrupt." Either method leads to failure, for either method eliminates the possibility of cure. Atoms are only atoms; recombine them as you will, they still remain atoms. If we could once say why a particular combination of atoms might be better than another, then we have gone beyond cynicism.

Likewise, if man is innately corrupt, no cure can be found. Everything that man touches and everything that touches man would amount to perversity. All turns to dirt, pulverized under the pressure of man's degenerate possessiveness and lust. What can be done in this situation? Absolutely nothing. There is no chance for redemption or change. For how would such a perverse creature be enlightened? If his mind is inevitably corrupt, there is no word which could penetrate that mind without turning into falsehood. And how would such a creature learn love? If his heart is inevitably sick, then any love directed to him would seem like sickness, and any love assayed by him would be playing charades. How could such a creature even accept salvation, for he would not, and could not, know his needs and what solution was being offered? How could he even know what a cure was?

In either case, meaningless atoms or meaningless corruption, reality simply is not met. If we are cynics, we cannot go about our daily work (for why would we do that), go about our daily living (for there would be no real point to that), or look a friend in the face (for friendship is truly impossible with cynicism), or dare to fall in love (for love without meaning is contradictory). The very things that we affirm in our daily life, the projects we undertake, the concerns we feel, the people we try to persuade, those we try to love, take the very punch out of our attempts at cynicism.

For no one really believes the best thing to be done with humans is to hope for annihilation so some new entity can perform better in man's place. Yet this is exactly what cynicism leads to.

To be true to ourselves, we must reject the urge to see things cynically. To reject the temptation of cynicism, we must believe in the spiritual energies of man. To believe in the spiritual energies of man, we must simply see what daily life is saying and take it for real.

For daily life shows points when our spiritual energies, our stabs at truth, our scrambling for love, emerge as the dominant force in our lives. I go to a movie not because I want to be diverted, but sometimes because I know the movie is beautiful. I am a person involved in beauty. I listen to an argument not always because I'm forced to, but at times I really want to understand. I am a person involved in truth. I approach another not merely because I want to manipulate him, but every once in a while I want to help, admire, cherish.

That we seek beauty, truth, love, that we want to be good or even perfect (somewhere in our fantasies), that we are restless for something deeper, something permanent, that we are highly complex people with very subtle needs—this does not refer to a new fairy tale about man but rather proffers to be the core of man's being. Take away these things, and the human project is utter nonsense, from the first instant of history to the last instant of our day.

In other words, the drives that distinguish man from all other reality cannot be renounced without ending up in the silly position of making a statement when no statement is appropriate because all is hopeless anyway. For all my baseness, I recognize my baseness as base. For all my deception, I want not to be deceived. For all my hate, I want to love. I could not know my baseness, deception, or my hate without first knowing and being defined by goodness, truth, and love.

If we want, we can play games. We can talk in terms of "instincts for survival," and "modifying man's behavior," and "finding the atomic structure of knowing," and "oedipus complexes," and "human projections," and "myths," and "determinism." But in the end we are really talking about hope, freedom, insight, development, perception, creativity, and destiny. We can use terms that reduce the human to quantity, but we do not really believe them. We know in our bones about a mystery far more staggering—the mystery of our human heart.

*

What I have been saying comes down to this: we cannot understand what we are all about if we (1) try to isolate man from man, or (2) doubt the spiritual and personal forces of man. Dally as we might with ideas of being the lone hero or nature's horrible trick, we cannot settle there and rest comfortably either with ourselves or with others. We are somehow forced to go about the business of life and this means seeing sense in our social nature and our personal nature.

What does this have to do with me as a believer? Quite simply, it tells me that, if we must take our social and personal natures seriously, then God probably will do so too. It tells me that a religious way of life that divorces me from a group, or undercuts the very thing it is trying to save, ultimately is inadequate— inadequate to me as a person and to a God who is Lord. If faith does not tie into our very communal life as human beings, then it is not for us. If faith does not promise and inculcate the transcendence of the human spirit, then it is not for mankind. Here are clues to human sense; here, therefore, are clues to religious sense —and to the sense of Catholicism.

Catholic sense says, in summary, that man was meant to be with man, to form community, to associate, to build, to live at peace. Catholic sense acknowledges that we are individuals, but individuals within a group that is essential for our individual life. It renounces the tendency to write off everyone else, for when everyone else is written off, so also are we. Further, Catholic sense takes the human at face value: there is no trick or illusion to man. His love is meant to be love, his knowing is meant to be correct, his searching is supposed to find fulfillment, his achievements are truly achievements. Catholic sense, then, also renounces the self-doubt that plays in the corner of man's mind, ready to sink the whole human project in a wave of self-pity.

Man is curable; man is not alone. These two fragile statements put into perspective a whole attitude on life, an attitude won with difficulty, an attitude which is crucial. Once we have mustered the courage or pain or gumption to dare to think we are not worthless, then we are in another world—the only world in which Catholicism is possible.

3 Salvation

Like all men, I'm a snooper. Like many people, I go snooping in different churches. Some go because they are searching. I go because I like to learn—I'm curious.

A friend and I went once to a small Baptist Church outside Washington, D.C., to hear a sermon on why it was sinful to baptize infants. The congregation sung with greater fervor than Catholics usually sing. Little children wiggled in the pews without being self-conscious. The adults put zest into everything: listening, praying, even the collection. And the preacher talked for more than half an hour on his subject. But the real high point was still to come.

It was not the sermon, the songs, the prayers, the readings, or the collection that was the climax of the service. Rather, it was the occasional calls for conversion that radiated every so often from the preacher: "Those who are ready to accept the Lord Jesus should step forward." A visitor might miss the import of these messages. Really, they were the key to the whole event.

Even when no one stepped forward, the minister did not seem bothered; he kept the service moving, biding his time. Sure enough, at the end of the ceremony, a couple did step forward.

They were old, grey, experienced. They walked slowly, almost wobbling, assisted by a deaconess who had intercepted them on the way. In what seemed an almost obscene manner (I had never seen anything like this before) they were crying—whimpers, sobs, handkerchiefs. Yet only a few of the congregation turned to watch; most just stared ahead. My friend and I watched with amazement. Questions raced through my mind: was this a regular happening? Was this manufactured drama, learned too well by the experienced congregation? A Sunday-morning soap-opera to atone for Sunday-afternoon football? Was it real?

It was real. The minister stepped down from the stage. He hugged first the man, then the woman. He asked them what they wanted. They blubbered out, "We want to be saved." He embraced them even more warmly, repeated their request louder for the benefit of the congregation, pointed out with exegetical clarity that the couple desired to abandon their way of sin and accept the Lord Jesus as their Savior. With saving grace, the couple was angled to other deaconesses and deacons who would aid them in the rites of passage from sin to sanctity.

*

"We want to be saved."

You bet we do! Every one of us has been pinned to the wall sometime or other in our lives. Whatever our religious disposition, we find ourselves yelling "Help," or "Save me," or "O my God," with almost embarrassing spontaneity.

Like when we've been rejected once too often without any obvious reason. Or when we learn that a friend is dead. Or when things have become so fuzzy we cannot even find the energy to cry. When we finally ask,

"What's the point?" When a lover says good-bye. Or when we cannot break a debasing habit. Or when we've just lost our temper once again without any reason.

In other words, life comes with its own built-in can opener. Some things are just too much pressure. Suddenly the can goes "phiss . . ." and everything is spilling on the sidewalk. We feel anger. We feel cheated. We are desperate. So we yell: "I want to be saved."

I've yelled it. Chances are excellent that you have yelled it, too. What were we yelling for?

It seems our first idea of salvation is to be freed from some particular threat or hardship. Some loss has happened or will happen, some terrible thing is upon us, and we beg to be *preserved*. We don't want the pain, the change, the loss. Salvation seems to be, at first sight, getting through a hard time, if only by the skin of our teeth.

If I were accepted, or my friend alive again, or the direction of my life more clear, or in better control of myself, more at peace, then I would be saved. My life would be mine once again. It would be back to normal.

But it never really goes back to normal. Once the can is opened, once the goods have spilled out, we have tasted the uncertainty that lies at the base of every second we live. We can pretend that things are back to normal, but we know, in our bones, they are not and never can be. Paradise lost.

Getting through a hard time then, seems to be only one part of what salvation means. For life goes on, wincing as it does, expecting, dreading, suppressing, speculating. The particular threat we felt was only one instance of a deeper threat, a more profound hurt, that chills the spine with subtle certainty.

The cry for salvation has, in fact, an echo about it.

On one level a voice goes out, but it keeps bouncing off different levels at various depths within us. For example, we are rejected seemingly without reason. Will this happen again? Will it happen all the time? What builds the walls between people, or bridges between people? Who establishes my worth? What am I really worth? The question goes on and on, solved for a while at one level, opening again at another level, calling into question the basis of life. And that—the very open-endedness of our fear—is the real heart of our call for salvation.

All of us feel a kind of "wrongness" to our lives. They do not go the way they should. Not only does life go wrong in terms of what we want; it goes wrong in our very planning and desiring. There is a problem with the whole of human existence.

Paradise lost. Even if we did not have a story of paradise with Adam and Eve, we all carry deep within ourselves some ideal picture of life which never occurs. We feel that life hobbles along out of step with itself. Our problem is a whole way of being; everything seems out of whack. Not just a particular act at one point of time, but our whole way of acting. Not just an inadequate thought on one topic or another, but our whole way of thinking. Not just a pressured situation here and now, but our whole existence.

What is the feeling? Generally, it seems to be a feeling that something is missing, something is lost, or something has not yet arrived.

We are tempted to think that death is the problem, but on reflection it seems to be only an occasion for meeting the problem. Death keeps me from knowing whether what was missing would ever have come. Death tells me that soon *I* shall be missing. It tells me that life is short. Because of this, it makes me painfully aware that I do not even know what to do with the short life that I have. Something is missing, and I do not know how to supply it or even whether I will have a chance to supply it. I do not even know for sure what I am lacking. Somehow, the problem is wrapped within me. It is not my death, but my life that seems lacking.

But the problem cannot be posed as "all is lost." To think that "all is lost" is merely to give way to futile cynicism which prevents any chance we have. Even though we fear that someday all could be lost, as long as we live we do not have that feeling. As long as we are, we sense there is a remedy. And as long as we sense there is a remedy, we are sensing that we are redeemable. For the instant we affirm that we are not redeemable, that nothing is worth saving, that "all is lost," then it is only a question of dotting "i's" and crossing "t's" in a pre-written script of life, for there is nothing to be gained or changed, no matter what we do.

Precisely because we have powers and capacities that resist defeat, we know that all is *not* lost. We know that we have something. We have a life, we can question and seek, wonder and love. We know our acts, irrational as they sometimes are, form a pattern that make up a story: we can build on that story, imagine it differently, affect it dramatically. We are not, then, in a totally negative situation. We have many positives. We are not a total loss. If we were, we would have no problem. One wastes no tears over a hopeless case.

The problem is not with death: it is with life. We feel that somehow, if we could find whatever is missing in our lives, death would not have the cruelty about it that it so often does. We also feel that if anyone could provide a solution to the "wrongness" of our lives, he could also provide a solution to death. For death can be viewed as part of the very human problem itself: an extreme manifestation, a finishing thrust, but still part and parcel with the innate sense that something is off kilter.

When we cry, "Save me," we are not merely asking for preservation. For even if we could preserve the life we have endlessly, the feeling of needed salvation would not recede. It would probably be heightened. We seek for truth, for a taste of reality, for an understood relationship with the world; all too often though, there is only haze, only insoluble question, only fleeting image. Even when we achieve truth, something still is missing, for not only does truth beget new questions prolifically, but it also leads us to over-reach: we define our inches as miles, intervene into all areas with a few learned techniques, imagine we have a new world when all we have is an old one in pieces. We take two steps, we think we have run a mile.

Something is needed because my insecurity breeds self-concern, but my self-concern breeds further insecurity. I desire to preserve and further myself; to do that, I am driven to concern for others. Yet my concern for others strikes against my self-preservation and self-assertion. Something is needed, for as often as I slip into love, I slip back again into the illusion that I am the center of the universe, that others are objects for my pleasure, for me. Something is missing in the strained love that pushes me to care so much about another that I would bend another's will where it will not go.

Whatever is needed, we meet its absence so often. Call us clowns, prophets, lovers, thinkers, liars, pretenders, rulers, spenders, organizers, criers, doubters, salesmen: whatever we are, we play our life against a backdrop that keeps vanishing, on a stage that has too many trick props.

If we boil it all down, it seems we cry for salvation because we live in a state of *frustration*. We live in-between. There is not total loss (for then there is no problem), nor is it total satisfaction (for then there is no problem either). We are delicately poised in-between, fingers in both the worlds of loss and satisfaction. This kind of life is best called frustration.

Frustration means that something expected does not come about. We have, for example, the goods to work things out right. We have the potential, the energy. Yet along with these capacities, there is the immediate prospect of failure (I may not meet my bills) and the long-range inevitability of unattainment (even if I pay all my bills, what have I done with my life). For goals may be attained at some points, at other points they may not; but over the long haul, they will not be ultimately attained, they will not bring final satisfaction. So expectation brings disappointment. Desire turns to frenzy. Plans turn to doodling. Things do not work out. We are frustrated.

It is our frustration that cries out for relief. Our ambivalent way of living (loss and satisfaction) demands resolution. We cry for salvation because we can see, but we see blurred; we can hear, but we hear confusedly; we can love, but never clearly. Like the painting on a canvas, like the land on which we stand, frustration affects all we do. Outsmart it, ignore it, conquer it with pyrrhic victories, it still defines our opening moves and defies our final, grandstand play.

If you have looked at yourself and sensed this innate frustration, then perhaps it will be possible to see salvation as only coming through *transformation.* Salvation is being transformed. When we cry to be saved, we are crying to be changed. We might want to be preserved from some danger at one point or another, but we really want to be transformed, for only radical change suffices for the encompassing, dominating, determining need we feel through the whole range of our life.

What can transformation offer us? It can offer us a way of looking for a solution to life that includes (1) annihilation, (2) preservation, and (3) novelty.

1) *Annihilation:* Being saved must include some annihilation because any change must contain some stopping, some ceasing-to-be. Change involves some taking away. From changing tubes to changing channels, we set aside what is not satisfactory to make room for what is. With our problem of frustration, what must be taken away is the sense of futility, of loss, of missing out on something. Whatever it is that makes our minds and methods go awry, whatever throws us out of kilter, must go.

2) *Preservation:* Being saved must include preservation, for if nothing is preserved, it hardly can be called saved. If our very nature and life is not being saved, then we cannot talk of human salvation. So if we seek a change in man, in his love or his mind, then that love and mind must endure through the change. Even if we scrape through the day, we are somehow saying we are worthwhile, we are redeemable. What we feel is redeemable must be preserved or else we've given up all hope. The need for preservation is merely the rejection of cynicism, for a cynic could never understand how

anything in man's nature would ever be worth preserving. If *I'm* going to be saved, *I* want to be around to experience it.

3) *Novelty:* Not only does change involve some taking away and some preservation, it also involves newness. Obviously, if we are the same absolutely before salvation as after salvation, then salvation has not taken place. Rather, something must be different. Something new must be brought into the equation. And this something, it seems, must come from beyond the powers of mankind, a change unaccountable from the energies of man. For if we could change ourselves, then we would not need salvation—just time. If we could change ourselves, then the whole human problem has been misread. If we could change ourselves, then it would be only a question of learning more, refining techniques, instilling proper habits. But we know this is not so. What is in question is the whole level of human existence, the whole context of any learning, any technique, any habit or act. This is why novelty is crucial to the human dilemma. For while novelty does not consist in a totally new being, it does consist in the total renewal of the being we call man.

*

What is attractive about *transformation* is the possibility of seeing a real change in man without losing the idea of man altogether. I do not want to be an angel, nor do I want my friends to be victims of their own salvation. If God has chosen to give us existence, human existence, then it only makes sense to think he appreciates his creation enough to want it to endure, to be fulfilled.

Transformation allows us to see the prospect of a new level of existence, a new state of energy for mankind. We are lifted from one field of being into a new field. The old field comprises the twisting and defeat of man's transcendent capacities; the new field comprises the ordering and fulfilling of those capacities. From stumbling love to generous life; from stuttering thought to truthful life; from broken existence to full life. As one field is defined from start to finish by frustration, the other field is defined from start to finish by transformation which leads to achievement, the achievement we seek with every movement of our lives.

I believe in man, as we all do. I believe in God, for God seems to me to be the purpose of man. I believe, further, in a God great enough to feel what we feel, the majesty and tragedy of our lives, and great enough to do something about our lives.

I believe in a God who takes enough care of us to want to transform us, and to begin that transformation in Jesus Christ. I believe this not merely because my own needs point to a solution like this, but because my experience of Jesus Christ tells me something like this is happening.

This is how Catholicism begins to make sense. For once we have rejected cynicism and come to a healthy grasp of the greatness of man, once we quit pushing God from our lives, then we are in a position to see a chance for change, a change that introduces unexpected and humanly unattainable novelty into our lives, a change that brings God's power into every fiber of our existence. When I see God and man crossed together, I see Christ. When I see God and mankind crossed together, I see the Catholic Church. If I believed neither in man nor in God, both attractive temptations at

times, then not only would I abandon the Church, I
would have to abandon the whole project of human life
as well.

To understand what a Catholic means by salvation, we need only grasp the fine problem enveloping
human existence. The problem is not one of total
worthlessness. Rather, it is the problem of being in the
middle, almost making something of ourselves but
never going the whole way, reaching enough to feel the
failure, searching enough to feel the loss; it is an equation half-finished. This is why the Catholic instinct
looks for man's salvation in his transformation. Part of
man's dilemma must be annihilated; the core of man's
being must be preserved; the scope of man's life must
be renewed. Man must be changed. We must be transformed.

If we have come far enough along to appreciate
the dilemma of man, then we have come far enough
along to try to face the Jesus who brings transformation.
Perhaps we are now ready to meet the Transformer.

4 The Transformer

Every once in a great while, we have the luxury of going back over our life, a kind of review of our personal history. Quiet moments in the summer sun, late night talks with a friend, incidental insights while filling out an application or writing a résumé.

At these times, we come across definitive moments that have permanently shaped us. Unexpectedly, we found ourselves engaged in something that became a lifelong project. Without forewarning, we stumbled onto another who taught us something of the meaning of life, or who became a lifelong partner. Perhaps we read a book, or went through a crisis, or traveled, or simply took the time to sit for a day or two: whatever, everything changed.

Of course, these things become clear with hindsight. We can look back and spot the crucial moments. Hardly ever could we spot them before they happened. Foresight brings a general picture, but only hindsight brings out the burning details and the central focus.

I can look back on my own life and pick out the moment that affected all others. I'm 17 years old, during a mid-afternoon slowdown in the lethargy of spring: Should I be a priest or not? My personality had been juggled around for a year or two as I struggled to set aside my own brand of protective cynicism and insecure cockiness. I had learned to like people. I had learned to love Christ. I wanted a way of life that was not "ordinary," in the sense that I wanted the rubber band to be pulled as hard as it could. Money was insignificant. Sex was not an overwhelming factor. Love was. Love shaping action. Love never stopping. Love bringing its peculiar blend of uneasy happiness. I had found this already, in my past religious life. I could look forward to this in a future religious life. Perhaps I could help. I definitely could grow. So why not?

Why that afternoon was different from any other afternoon of musing is a mystery. Nothing particularly prepared me for it. Only the following years made it into a turning point. I'm still living on the gas received at that particular fill-up.

All of us are, knowingly or not, living off the insights of a few central moments which careful looking back will open to us. It sometimes hurts to look back, for the essential ingredient in a "definitive moment" is that our life *has been shaped*. Unrepeatable, unescapable, we are its product or its victim. We fantasize what it would be like if we had chosen otherwise—where would I be, what would I be doing, what would I be? But these are fantasies. What we *are* is real.

*

Because foresight is so much more inferior than hindsight, there is built-in danger in approaching Jesus Christ. That danger rests in our personal anticipations of salvation. It also rested in the collective pile of anticipations which beset the Jews of Jesus' time. After all, we feel if we can analyze our situation carefully enough, learn the precise problems, then it would be no difficulty at all to imagine a savior who will bring relief to these problems. So we project answers—but the actual solution might be quite different from our projection.

In fact, for all the value of anticipating salvation, it simply cannot be done. And the simple reason is that we *are* dealing with salvation. If we have probed the frustration of our lives deeply enough, then we know that salvation cannot come from us, that it must come from beyond our powers—even our powers to conceptualize. Whatever difficulties we experience in human nature, the solution to these difficulties always escapes us. When it comes to salvation, we are *receivers*. After all, whatever dabbling we have done in religion, any dabbling is sufficient to convince us God cannot be out-guessed. God's transcendence has surprise wrapped within it. God is unpredictable, salvation is novel.

All this makes understandable the reluctance of Jesus' contemporaries to accept him. With many projections of what their expected savior might be like, Jesus fit none of those projections exactly. They did not have the advantage of hindsight as we do.

And even with our advantage, until we have experienced Jesus, we tend to miss him. We want him to do certain things for us: give us good feelings, provide moral strength, protect us from uncertainty, even produce a miracle in a pinch. So we color our picture of a savior and try to force Jesus into it.

But the savior eludes our projections and manipulations. He comes to bring what we vaguely suspect. He comes with his own fullness and integrity. After all, we are dealing with God and man. Much as we attempt to map out the intricacies of human nature and the human dilemma, those intricacies escape our complete understanding; even more, the subtlety and simple depth of God make our hearts stand numb. What are we really

like? What is God really like? How does God go about
working with us and in us?

It's quite a problem. What word should God use in
addressing us? What sign will make him unmistakably
clear? Lighting flashes, or computer read-outs, disas-
ters, or lavish wealth? God, after all, is not just an ordinary next-door neighbor. So how does he get through
to us?

First, we need preparation. God has to prepare us.
God has to do what he did among the Jews, building a
people and a culture that became used to his words and
deeds, that expected him, that yearned for him. Need-
less to say, some preparation for God takes place in our
own lives as well. Fluctuating between disappointment
and hope, we learn to keep our eyes open, to stand
alert, sharpened by anticipation. God braces us.

But no bracing guarantees success. More than
once in our lives we have missed what lies before our
very noses. Think about the aborted opportunities, the
miscalculated moves, the thousands of trees we have
wrongly barked up! Prophet after prophet might make
his point, induce enthusiasm, call for reform; incident
after incident might make us think, show the futility of
our lives, beg for a change of direction. But prophets
pass and incidents pass. Even were the prophets perfectly clear, even were our experiences absolutely unam-
biguous, we still would pull back. Like staring into the
sun, gazing at God produces a natural squinting.

So there is no surprise that when Christ appeared
among us the foresight of the Jews was simply inadequate. The thrust is too bold: God and man working
together, intricacy wound in brilliance, the inexpressible now encoded in flesh. It is simply too much! The

message is too stark, the Christ is too direct. No wonder that we, like the Jews, toy around with him and then pull away; the bait seems too powerful.

Like a double helix knotted upon itself, the richness of Jesus proved excessive. Approach him any way you want, there is always more to unravel, to pick at, to play with, to wonder about. Jesus causes wonder today, even as he did then. And wonder, if pursued, takes work; perhaps more work than we want to put out. Again, God is not our ordinary next-door neighbor.

But there he stands, the "decisive moment" ripping into our foresight and our hindsight, a critical event that either shapes us or misshapes us. We look at him from different directions. The testimonies about him, reflecting his richness, weave back and forth in convoluted strands. He is man leading us to God; he is God leading us to man. He talks to us in plain language; he talks to us in mystery. He walks along roads touching the blind, then he blinds his apostles in transfiguration. He seems to be a searcher, but a searcher who has already found. He appears to be a struggler, but a struggler confident of the outcome, a struggler in the hands of glory.

There he stands, so many pieces and clues dropped into our lap in almost cruel generosity. And what do we do? What now?

Somehow, we are forced into the tangled mystery of Christ to find out what salvation means for us, to find out what kind of salvation God offers us in Christ. We have to grab a strand and start pulling, start unraveling, trusting that if we are knotted in, we will be better for it. And the strand to pull on is the strand of our

identity with Christ, our humanity, for this is our starting point in everything. It is humanity that must be
saved. If Christ brings and embodies salvation for us,
then the place of transformation will be exactly in his
human nature. If we can understand what happens to
Jesus' human nature which exists in such intimate
union with God, then we can get a glimpse of the kind
of transformation God offers to all of us through union
with him.

Here we come upon a cardinal point in Christian
and Catholic thought: *God saves the human through
the human.* The manhood of Jesus is where we learn
what salvation means for mankind. Here is God taking
our human nature seriously. This is God's renunciation
of cynicism. This is how he values the humanity he
created. He encodes himself in it. He takes it to himself. He becomes one of us. Through one of our own,
we discover salvation, the Savior, the saving God. Of
all the possible combinations God might have tried, he
throws this combination at us: God enmeshed in our
flesh.

A combination that still is too much for us—that
we often want to take apart. All of us who are children
of the enlightenment believe so much in the ordinary
that we strip the unusual, the novel, of its extraordi-
nariness, so it will be understandable, common sense,
within our reach. So we want to go after Jesus with sur-
gical tools, severing the "superstitious" so thoroughly
that we end up with "someone like us"—not only
human like us, but untransformed like us. We think a
picture of an "ordinary Jesus" (no miracles, especially,
no grandeur, no cryptic remarks) far more preferable
than the one we have to work with.

This, of course, is another way of manipulating a

"decisive moment," to fill out *our* expectations and demands. It may ease our understanding, even make us feel less gullible; it may also keep us going in a perfect circle, ending up where our presuppositions started, leaping from "ordinary life" back to "ordinary life" without any insight at all.

There is, really, only one Jesus that we have to work with, only one "decisive moment" presented by those who testify to him. That Jesus stands before our eyes as he did before the Jews' eyes, intriguing and baffling at the same time. We cannot paint another picture of Jesus and still be faithful to him because the picture we have, preached and proclaimed by the apostles, recorded in the scriptures, *is* the representation of their experience, *is* what they saw and heard.

What the apostles saw and proclaimed was Jesus' humanity in various stages of transformation. They did not see his "divinity" as if they had some emotional gold paint to dab into his picture. Divinity cannot be seen; it is beyond human vision, nonphysical, nonmaterial. The effect of divinity in human life can be seen, what God was doing when joined to one of us. That is the apostolic report. That is what jars our nerves and our imagination.

And that is what the believer wants to grasp. If we want to see Jesus untransformed, ordinary like us, then we can strip away all we will, demonstrating only a remarkable analytic ability but missing the point of Christ. The believer, though, has only the task of gazing, of understanding the very transformation that Jesus came to bring, the very change that was his mission. The baffling and disturbing picture of Christ forces us to look exactly where we should look. Jesus shared our own untransformed nature and at the same time was bringing novelty to our untransformed nature through the transformation of his life. This *is* exactly the clue: eliminate it at your own risk!

What is the scope of transformation that Jesus brings us? We can try to decipher his life by looking for the kind of annihilation, preservation, and novelty that he embodied during his life. In this way, we have access to the critical moment that he presents us with.

*

Annihilation refers to the negative side of any transformation, the ceasing that must take place in any change. Something present must be eliminated and negated. Otherwise, there is no change.

Christ reverses forces of failure both within and outside of man. Within man there is a whole way of acting and thinking which has to cease if man is to be transformed. "Unless your holiness surpasses that of the scribes and Pharisees, you shall not enter the kingdom of God" (Matt. 5:20). By "holiness" Jesus is referring to a total mentality, a whole way of discerning, a complete sense of "rightness," which must exceed the best available at that time, that of the scribes and Pharisees. For, much as Jesus attacked the scribes and Pharisees, their moral tone and religious fervor were quite high. Jesus points here to a complete perspective which we must have on life.

Parable after parable, Jesus exposes the laziness and listlessness which poison our human spirit. He countered our hesitation with parables of daring—the man who invests all he has to buy a field containing hidden treasure (Matt. 13:44). He countered man's fear of God with the story of the prodigal son who returns not to a frightening Father but to a Father who longs to embrace his lost son (Luke 15:11-31). Our cowering before hardship received a sharp rejoinder in the parable of the Good Samaritan who did not recoil from involvement in robbery and possible murder, even when the victim was considered a traditional enemy (Luke 10:30-36).

Boldly, Jesus strikes at the very insecurity that besets all mankind—the worry and fretting about life and possessions. What must cease is our very concern about our life, our sustenance, our body, our clothes (Luke 12:22). God's care far exceeds our own, our final security rests in him (Matt. 6:30ff). This is why the poor, the sorrowing, the weak, and the persecuted are truly blessed: they have given up the clinging and grasping that produce much tension but not much else. They have a freedom to be seized by God's kingdom (Matt. 5:3-12).

This mentality, which Jesus undercuts, runs throughout the range of our spirit. It spawns the frustration that we feel in human life—the nervous clutching that generates only cramps. For worry brings us nothing but worry; we attempt to build our own security only to realize how insecure we really are.

But this mentality also arises from being possessed by a different force, a power that encircles our whole environment, a domination, a slavery, which Jesus called the kingdom of Satan. "I saw Satan fall from the sky like lightning!" Jesus exclaims in triumph (Luke 10:18). Satan's force was present every moment to Jesus, but as a force outside him, a force that he never let touch him, a force that was to be conquered. While Satan steals the word that Jesus came to bring (Mark 4:15), Satan has already been mastered by Christ.

"Away, Satan," Jesus squelches his temptations: Jesus' life was to be lived not in terms of manipulation, political power, or crowd-pleasing. Rather, he would live in terms of his Father in heaven (Matt. 4:310). Satan represents the decision to live without God at the center of our lives; Satan's kingdom, the snaring web of this decision, is locked in unrelenting confrontation with Jesus. No compromise is possible. When Jesus cast out demons with his own power, he shows the end of evil's domain (Mark 3:23).

In almost all his movements, Jesus signifies the overthrow of man's listlessness and Satan's dominion. This is the meaning of the healings, the casting out of demons, the raisings from the dead. This is the effect of the "change of heart" Jesus demanded and induced in his mission of correcting and healing.

Both our insecurity and Satan's power come into play in Jesus' ultimate act of annihilation—who the annihilation involved in his death and resurrection. It is Satan who enters into Judas and begins the destiny which part of Jesus' lot (Luke 22:3; John 13:16). It is likewise the calculating insecurity of Jewish leaders that made the death of Jesus look attractive, good, and necessary. "It is only right that one man die for the people," Caiphas, the chief priest, explains (John 11:49-50). His reasoning is clear and almost frighteningly indefensible: either Jesus goes or the Jewish nation goes. He must intervene, take matters into his own hands, figure things out in starkly realistic terms if the Jewish nation is to survive. Certainly, he wasn't going to leave anything up to God!

So death becomes the final test case. Jesus takes upon himself the full force of what could be thrown against him. The mistakenly noble attitude of the religious leaders, the perverse forces that dominate the human heart, the envy, fear, and hatred latent behind so many human acts are all crystallized in the drama of Jesus' death. This is the final lunge, the last stand. Jesus' whole life and preaching are at stake in this. If death wins, if his mission is frustrated, not only does evil win, but also the ultimate evidence of human frustration wins. Reality would be exposed for the shell it is.

Death lost. The extreme instance of human frustration, the culmination of man's blindness and Satan's power, busted open. In rising from the dead, Jesus shows not only the ceasing of death, but also the ceasing of man's failure and futility.

Christ offers us the annihilation of those factors that work to our frustration. He clears the board of the negative and debilitating fibers in our makeup. This is the first aspect of the transformation he came to bring about; it is the first part of what we understand as salvation. Salvation entails the stopping of blindness, frustration, failure, sin, the domination of evil, and, finally, death.

*

The second aspect of transformation is preservation—the continuity that must be present in any change. If there is no continuity, then we simply have an end and a beginning with no connection between. The very thing we try to save would be destroyed. Just as the human race cannot at the same time be destroyed and transformed, so Jesus, in whom transformation subsists, cannot be destroyed and bring transformation without contradiction. For this reason, scripture contains the insight, "Jesus Christ is the same, yesterday, today, and forever" (Heb. 13-8).

If we see mankind as redeemable and having worth, then we must insist on some preservation and continuity. In Jesus, God subsumed the same human reality, the same potential, the same existence that begs for salvation and transformation. Here lies the crux of the doctrine of the incarnation: in Jesus, God saves the flesh that is doomed on its own by becoming one with it. We can hope for our transformation because of the transformation of human nature in Jesus Christ.

We can make sense out of the salvation of Jesus only if we see a double continuity: first, a continuity between Jesus' human reality before and after his resurrection, throughout the various levels of his own transformation; and secondly, a continuity between the human reality of Jesus and us. He is and remains one of us.

The shock of having God enfleshed with us has pushed some religious thinkers to protect God by severing him from Jesus' humanity; Jesus as a human was only a mirage, or a borrowed instrument or something like that: God merely appeared incarnate, but he was not really so! Believers resisted this kind of thinking forcefully because to sever God from man in Christ, or to sever Christ from man in our shared human nature, would destroy the whole fabric and meaning of salvation. Deny Jesus a real body, or deny his real human understanding, or his real human choosing; but do so only at the risk of leaving our bodies, our understanding, our human choosing outside the very transformation God is working. What is untransformed in Christ must be untransformed in us as well. God saves what he joins himself to.

This is the logic behind the narratives of Jesus' resurrection in which he shows the apostles his wounds, has them touch him, eats before them. He is demonstrating that humanity is capable of existing, through God's power, at various stages and levels of being. Further, he is showing that these different levels of being can all belong to us, who are his brothers. "This is what we are proclaiming—what has existed from the beginning, what we have heard, what we have seen with our eyes, what we have looked upon, what we have touched" (1 John 1:1).

*

Change involves newness, novelty. If all is the same at the beginning and the end, then there is no change. In our quest for transformation, novelty refers to the change which comes about that cannot be explained by the latent powers and forces of our nature. We cannot save ourselves. So we are not dealing here with a seed and its future plant or some process in which each step generates the next.

Instead, in our transformation, the novelty must be radical, touching our roots. For the problem of human existence lies in our lack of true novelty: for all our progress, the human condition has been passed on from generation to generation intact. Our thorough frustration—the unfulfilled expectations, the dissipated energies—demands novelty for its correction.

This means more than a simple return to some "Garden of Paradise" in which the negative aspects of our existence (ignorance, death, weakness of will, insecurity, etc.) are eliminated. For much as we might daydream of a return to some pristine state of innocence and joy, we really need more than this—and God has revealed something more than this. To return, after all, to early innocence only opens up the possibility of failing once again. No one with any self-knowledge actually thinks he would do better than Adam! We need more than a return; we need a renewal.

Yet how do we talk of novelty, we who have not experienced it, or have experienced only its beginnings? Even the experience that the apostles had of Jesus risen in glory could not bring about full comprehension or clear expression. For the novelty involved in the transformation of Jesus Christ was the working of the transcendent God in our world. Insofar as Jesus' human nature was transfused with the power of God, it partakes of God's transcendent action, which outstrips all our descriptive capacities.

This is why there is a whole spectrum of terms used to identify Christ. Prophet, teacher, He-who-is-to-come, Messiah, Son of God, Lord: all these attempt to come to grips with the transformed nature of Christ— transformed by virtue of Jesus' sharing in God's nature as risen Lord.

Lord—the description we found of God in our first chapter—seemed a satisfactory term for the novelty of Christ. St. John's Gospel culminates in the confession of the now-unskeptical Thomas, who utters, "My Lord and My God" before the risen Christ (John 20:28). Peter cries out at the Transfiguration, "Lord, how good it is to be here!" because gazing on the glory of Jesus fulfilled in anticipation profound religious longings in man. Paul summarizes the faith of the early Christians in the encompassing three-word formula: "JESUS IS LORD!" (Rom. 10:9) A hymn already in use before Paul incorporated it into his letter to the Philippians culminates in the same profession: "JESUS CHRIST IS LORD!" (Phil. 2:11)

This term is trying to hit at the condensed meaning of Jesus. Even when he is crucified, Jesus is "Lord of Glory" (1 Cor. 2:8). There is an encompassing quality about Jesus that makes him heart of all that is and master of all the cosmos. He is the focal point of God's plan "to bring all things on heaven and earth under Christ's headship" (Eph. 1:10). Jesus, as Lord, attains priority and centrality in creation.

He is God's image, the first of all creatures, the one for whom all things were made, the one whose power guides even the making of things, prior to everything, in whom everything continues to exist. "It pleased God to make absolute fullness reside in him and, by means of him, to reconcile everything in his person" (Col. 1:15-19). There is nothing that lies outside the scope of Christ. He has dominion over all.

He is the secret latent in the universe which explains the universe. Lordship means that Jesus Christ, in his humanity, is taken into the divinity of God in a full and effective way so that God's transcendence and power over all is now exercised in Christ. Jesus radiates the "glory" of God—the brilliance akin to God's self-manifestation. Lordship is Jesus' living in unrestrictedness: life, wisdom, power, beauty, joy, peace, love, such as we have needed and longed for, are his in every dimension without limit. "The Lamb that was slain is worthy to receive power and riches, wisdom and strength, honor and glory and praise!" (Rev. 5:12)

We can be easily misled here, thinking that Jesus is Lord because he is divine. Rather, the apostles perceived Jesus as Lord, sharing in the transcendent power of God, before they began to understand how Jesus shared in the Father's life. His Lordship appeared more clearly than his divinity; time and adjustment brought his divinity into focus later on.

Lordship, then, is not merely ascribed to Jesus as divine; it is ascribed to Jesus as a human being. It is far too easy to slip into an attitude that makes Jesus non-human. To do that destroys the point of his being Lord, and also the point of our transformation. For our hope of transformation lies in Jesus' human nature; as a human, Jesus is Lord. As humans, we too may share in his Lordship.

Jesus' Lordship can be expanded in two directions that influence the two basic elements of human nature, our understanding and our action. In this light, Jesus comes to be seen as *wisdom*, Lord of our understanding, and *power*, Lord of our action.

One of the pivotal points of Matthew's Gospel is the Sermon on the Mount. The messages of this sermon, scattered throughout Luke's Gospel, are collected together by Matthew into one majestic discourse. Jesus instructs on the mount, as God himself instructed the Jews in the Old Testament through Moses, who gave the law which was at the heart of Jewish life. Jesus is the new Law, the new Wisdom, bringing the enlightenment of God to men. "Jesus finished his sermon and left the crowds spellbound at his teaching. The reason was that he taught with authority and not like their scribes" (Matt. 7:28-29).

Throughout his ministry, Jesus attempted to bring the apostles directly into another way of thinking. "To you the mystery of the kingdom is confided. To others outside it is all presented in parables" (Mark 4:11). The apostles can see the mystery—the secret, the revelation

—of God's kingdom because they are living with that revelation itself: they are living with Jesus. Even so, he is too much for them. They, too, need the parables to be gradually brought into Jesus' mentality. When the apostles' lack of understanding is noted (cf. Mark 6:25), this is a way of contrasting Jesus' wisdom with the shallow wisdom of those whose minds are not yet transformed.

As Jesus is the paragon of existence in his Lordship, he is the paragon of understanding in his wisdom. St. Paul argues this very closely in his first letter to the Corinthians. Paul notes that only our own spirit really knows ourselves. "Who, for example, knows a man's innermost self but the man's own spirit within him?" Our attempt to gain intense knowledge of another has limits. In the same way, we cannot know the depths of God—except that God's Spirit is given to us. Only by a special participation in God's innermost depths can we know God intimately. "But we have the mind of Christ," Paul says (1Cor. 2:11-16). It is in Christ that we attain participation in God's Spirit, the Spirit that Jesus as Lord sends into our hearts, bringing us into the life of God.

In other words, Christ becomes our wisdom. The knowledge that he brings us dominates our minds, unfolds our understanding, transforms our mentality. We come to see differently, to know differently. Christ brings a "whole new way of thinking" to those who share in his transforming knowledge. The knowledge that we have in Christ permeates every fiber of our minds in a comprehensive vision of reality in terms of what is most real—in terms of Christ. This is why Paul wishes his converts to be "enriched with full assurance by their knowledge of the mystery of God—namely Christ—in whom every treasure of wisdom and knowledge is hidden" (Col. 2:3).

So Jesus is ultimately seen as "The Word"—the Mind, the Intelligence which is God himself and which lies behind everything (John 1:1). Jesus embodies truth, embodies what is real: "I am the way, the truth, and the life," Jesus proclaims. (John 14:6) It is our loss of contact with reality that causes us to misread Jesus and flee when we should be awestruck: "Because I deal in the truth, you give me no credence." (John 8:45). If Jesus is the light of the world, then all which is outside of him is in some kind of darkness.

That darkness we have all felt. That is why he comes as the light which darkness, even ours, cannot quench. (John 1:5).

Jesus appears not only as Wisdom, but also as power. As men asked where Jesus got his wisdom, they also wondered where he acquired his powers (Matt. 13:54). When the paralytic is brought before him to be cured, with calm authority Jesus astonishes the crowd with a cure of the man's body and forgiveness of his sins. "They were awestruck; all gave praise to God, saying, 'We have never seen anything like this!'" (Mark 2:12) Again and again, Jesus shows his power over many different afflictions of mankind. He shapes situations according to God's will, bringing about the irruption of the kingdom of God into human affairs.

Equal with his cures, there is the shaping force he exercised on people's lives. The strength of his personality draws fishermen to abandon their livelihood at his invitation (Mark 1:16-20). He converses with the Samaritan woman and changes her life (John 4:4-42). He approaches Matthew with the direct "Follow me," and Matthew leaves a network of associates and finances to pursue this startling person (Matt. 9:9-10). In desperation, the religious enemies of Jesus tell of his success, wondering how it could be stopped: "What are we to do with this man performing all sorts of signs? If we let him go on like this, the whole world will believe in him" (John 11:47-48).

As Paul sees it, Jesus is designated Son of God "in power" (Rom. 1:4). Christ is power for salvation, for transformation. The powerlessness of human effort to effect any real change in human life finds rescue in the power of Jesus Christ, who stands against the manifold powers which entrap man, the powers of the world, of sin, of death. Christ's power in and through his followers is immeasurable (Eph. 1:19). For the power he has to lay down his life and take it up again means ultimately the power to sway our lives so much that we partake in his own resurrection (John 10:17-18).

What we make of all this depends partly on us and partly on Christ. The decisive moment of Christ can become a decisive moment for us, if we dare to see here a symbol, and, more, an embodiment of salvation.

It depends on us because we can keep on going the way we have been going, making the kind of sense that has worked so far. This amounts to saying that we need no salvation, or salvation is not possible, or salvation is not connected with Christ. To say we need no salvation means we are easily contented or our experiences are severely limited. To say salvation is not possible means we have really given up on ourselves and our race. To say salvation is not connected with Christ means we have found it somewhere else.

I find it, however, in Christ because I am not promised escape, or easy fulfillment, or esoteric magics, or empty humanistic phrases. I find it in Christ because I am promised fulfillment in my human nature, the humanity in which I have come to know and to love. I find it in him because evil is not illusioned away, nor is goodness cynically dismissed. In him there is the clash that takes place at least in me and probably in all men: the clash between meaning and meaninglessness, frustration and fulfillment, death and life.

What we make of Christ depends on him, and not only on us. Because Christ's Lordship means he still acts, he transforms now, attracts now, saves now. None of us can escape his influence. He will let none of us pass by without some notice, some call to greatness, some hunger for life.

Salvation seems possible for us; we make no sense without it. God seems capable of saving us, and he makes no sense without trying. Christ seems to be the critical point where God and man touch in painful, blissful ecstasy, each joining the reality of the other. That this must happen somewhere in our existence makes sense; that this has happened in Christ thrills the believer's spirit.

Here is a rare opportunity: to choose a decisive moment, to blend foresight and hindsight into an act that says "Yes" to Christ. Risky? Of course. Despite all the foresight and hindsight we can have into our need for Christ and our experience of him, where he takes us still is unknown, still will never be known until we are transformed in him. The unknown always seems risky. But to miss taking this risk might mean missing the key we've fumbled around for years trying to find.

5 Transformation

Getting it all together. . .

That's what we were doing in the 1960's. We felt that unbelievable feeling of utopia sweep through us. John the President and John the Pope opened up the sizzling pot and found out kernels were popping under the quiet of the 1950's. Kernels popping all over the place: ideas, questions, dreams, proposals, meetings, legislation. . . . .

Getting it all together; quite a job in those frantic years, a job for the country and a job for ourselves. We had to make decisions at every turn: Do I stand for ecumenism (let me think what that means for a minute, will you?); and am I willing to be arrested for what I think? Was I liberal or conservative? Would I *really* mind if my daughter married a black? What kind of nuclear deterrent did we need, how many megatons, how many megadeaths?

The questions rolled before us with such persistence that we often wondered what we thought, what our own place in all this was. Perhaps we toyed with joining the Peace Corps, or Vista, or working in Appalachia, or setting up some government program under the Office of Economic Opportunity, or the United Poverty Office, or some such wild-sounding but important organization. Perhaps we numbed the afternoons away with records by Joan Baez or Bobby Dylan, Simon and Garfunkel, or Buffy St. Marie—records that exposed the shallow world we wanted to destroy with the fire of reform.

Popping kernels and shallow worlds—two alternatives that pulled us apart. The shallow world of suburban security revolted us; but the world of popping kernels had no security about it at all except the certainty of another question, another cause, another reason to die.

Maybe we went looking for some therapy of one sort or another, some encounter group or authentic experience when at least we could know what we were dealing with. (Do you feel anger? Yes. How does it feel? Wonderful! At least I can feel something definite.) Touch my hand, someone, let me know I'm not alone. I've got to work through this or that, just give me time. Let me dream of a Peace Corps assignment; let me listen to my records; let me make a thousand pilgrimages to different concerts where fellow-puzzlers can mingle in freedom, away from the establishment, away from the world, away from making a decision.

How do I get it together? How does it tie into one bundle? How do I get it all into a manageable, digestible question? Or do the issues digest me?

So we sought for our identity: you and I wandering through the Sixties, just before the cataclysm of Vietnam, committed, engaged, searching, and wondering who we were. Our commitments shifted every couple of months, our interests, our causes. Or maybe they stayed the same, but we shifted from enthusiasm to intelligent distance to learned skepticism, finally ending in indifference.

We all have had those moments when nothing fit together, when we felt like smoke hanging in the air, pointless, positionless, part of the scenery. All this energy—and we haven't the slightest idea how to spend it. All this laziness—and nothing jolts us out of it. Ideas don't connect. Actions don't meet with results. Plans don't turn into anything. People stare at each other without even knowing it.

These moments and that era, I suppose, were good for us because we were somehow forced to seek connections in our lives, or at least to recognize our need for them. We discovered that a life not tied together was a hell of a life; an untied life gradually tied itself in unknown ways to addictions that were subtle or gross.

If we are at all religious now, it is probably because religion helped us tie enough things into a sensible arrangement during a time of turmoil. If our concerns were with the larger questions of politics or the pressing questions of personal meaning, we somehow toyed around with the worth of man and the strength of God to sift the more grotesque fantasies from our minds. Doubt, after all, can get to the hardest of us, turning our stomachs at the sight of ourselves, overturning success into questionable failure, blurring the difference between love and hate.

Getting it all together, or at least getting enough together, is a central function of all religious and the dominant interest of Catholicism. No one, for example, can look at a cathedral without being hit at every level by the amount that it pulls together. The personal lives of men given in erecting such a sweeping building, the stones and pillars joining in delicate juggling, the historical events leading to and enshrined in the church, the tones of light and dark, the colors of stained glass which compound biblical stories and worldly figures in an ordered kaleidoscope, monsters and saints hanging from doorways, the very edifice a prism separating and contracting dozens of strands of human existence—and all of this an attempt to symbolize the personal triumph of each Christian moving through life to fulfillment.

Whether symbolized in a cathedral or a book or a relationship with a friend, we need something that ties the loose ends of our lives together into something with a purpose and a point. We need enough faith and meaning to stare doubt down, to boil laziness away, to direct energy. We need to see the connection between those "decisive moments" of our lives and the events that follow. We need to see a connection between the life of Christ and our lives. We need to see a connection between ourselves and our fellow-man.

*

"The spirit of the Lord fills the world, is all-embracing" (Wisdom 1:7). This passage has been applied in Catholic worship to the Holy Spirit, and this application is a fair description of the Holy Spirit as experienced in Christians throughout the Church's history. For the Spirit connects us with Christ. To determine that Jesus brings us transformation, after all, is different from determining *how* that transformation affects us, historically so distant from him. Jesus' power, wisdom, and Lordship must be shared by us: this is the very point of salvation. This sharing is the work of the Spirit.

The Spirit ties together what Christ did and is with our actions and lives. The Spirit also ties together the levels of each life, bringing our diverse thoughts and actions into focus. The Spirit, shared by many, also ties together a people who belong in the same sphere of influence.

Paradoxically, though, scholars have always had difficulty tying the Spirit together and pinning him down. He has always been the most difficult aspect of God to grasp. Scholars wonder to what extent St. Paul was able to appreciate the difference between the risen Christ and his Spirit. Paul writes in one place, "The Lord is the Spirit, and where the Spirit of the Lord is, there is freedom. All of us, gazing on the Lord's glory with unveiled faces, are being transformed from glory to glory into his very image by the Lord who is Spirit" (2 Cor. 3:17-18). Yet, in other places, Paul seems to show a distinct difference with his frequent phrase, "The Spirit of the Lord."

Is Paul confused? Not really. Paul writes from personal experience, and the action of the Spirit lies precisely in this personal experience. In the Spirit, Paul encounters Jesus. The Spirit is the instrument of Jesus' risen presence, the power of Christ pulsing in the Christian. How do we separate the rays of light from the light itself? Each is inseparably bound up in the other. So Jesus and his Spirit.

What does the Spirit do? He is the running energy of Christian life, the very movement of any Christian action. The Spirit illumines, consoles, strengthens, makes holy, guides, binds together, commands, empowers: he brings, in short, human life into the transformed sphere of Jesus Christ.

If he does all this, why is the Spirit hard to grasp? Just because he does all this! The spirit works so close to us that his nearness makes him difficult to acknowledge. Think, for a moment, about your thinking and choosing. We do these things all the time, but we never allude to them. When we think, we think; we don't think about our thinking. When we choose and act, we bring about a goal; we don't ponder the internal and external steps to a goal unless we are forced to.

It's the same with the Spirit. We do not allude to him precisely because his work is so extensive and so intensive that he becomes inseparable from our very actions. Like the smile on a face, or the vibrations of a phonograph needle, or the swing of a bat: inseparable, entwined, acting, enabling. So it is only natural to bypass this subtlest aspect of God. When things are tied together, we simply don't stop to gaze at the binding force.

Chiseled, molded, pulled, refined, filed-down, built-up, we are made, by the Spirit, into the "very image" of Christ—so that his thoughts become ours and ours his, his actions ours and our actions his. This makes the drama of Christ's death and resurrection, with the transformation he embodied, into a fulcrum of our own lives, so that we become what he is. No longer a gripping tale arousing our sympathy, the story of Christ becomes autobiography.

And the range of the Spirit *is* comprehensive— "all-encompassing," as the Book of Wisdom puts it. There is nothing outside the Spirit's range except sin. The whole social reality of Christian life, the whole personal reality of a Christian life, in all its aspects and intricacies, is the range of the Spirit of God, the scope of transformation. For the God who creates, creates everything; the God who saves, saves what he creates. One cannot draw lines around parts of human life and say God has no place there. One cannot build walls around reality and say that Jesus will not work there. One cannot isolate elements of the human universe and exclude the Spirit. For the Lordship of Jesus means that everything falls under his sway.

This is an essential point of Catholic thinking. Everything belongs under Christ in his Spirit. This idea has shaped the Christian mind from the formation of the earliest Christian communities, on through the composing of the Gospels, the formation of an elaborated Christian teaching, the tough Christian who went to the desert to live, the lavishness of Byzantine worship, the genius of Roman and western organization, the bold missionary thrusts into "barbarian territory," the erection of churches, the development of Christian theology, the education of Christian people, the founding of religious communities, the impetus for Christian reform, the struggle for Christian values—the whole gamut of Christian culture. All is the work and effect of the Spirit.

For some, the idea of Christian culture seems contradictory. Culture is evil and depraved; Christianity saves us from it (flee the world!). For the Catholic, unless Christianity abides in and through a culture in all its reachings, then Christianity does not really yet exist. We cannot have humanity without a culture; we cannot have a saved humanity without a transformed culture.

We may never get it all together in our lives. This need not bother us if we have enough together not to fear what will come, to be able to make sense out of the patches of our lives, to face the future without cringing. For getting it together is a big step in the transformation we seek, the change from insecure listlessness to mature achievement. Getting it together is also pat of what Jesus offers us in his Spirit. The one who does not gather with him, scatters (Matt. 12:30). A scattered life is the kind of life that makes us beg for salvation in the first place.

Midword

Permit me to have a little word in the middle of this book. A little word to say we've passed halfway, perhaps not in pages, but in ideas.

If you have followed with me this far, then you admit certain things that all religious men admit, and other things that most Christians admit. You admit that God's power is his, outstripping our attempts to grasp it or manipulate it. You admit that man is a hopelessly social animal who cannot stand alone as a single atom in a horrible void. You further admit that you have not given up on mankind: he's lovable, worthwhile, redeemable.

Being redeemable, however, means being transformable: mankind can be changed to live up to the tremendous potential within him. We don't want to destroy him; we don't want to start all over; we don't want to keep him exactly as he is. We want to change him, good old *homo sapiens*.

Jesus Christ comes before us as an opportunity for such change. He is a decisive moment for mankind, for he offers us the possibility of destroying the destructive elements within us, preserving the core of us, transforming the powers of us. His own life can be seen as the process of transformation unveiled before us. His risen life is so startling and shattering that it affects all men: he is the turning point of our race and can be the turning point of our personal lives.

How? Through his Spirit which he sends on us in his risen power and glory so that we can become what he is—so we can share in his Lordship as he is Lord, share in his wisdom as he is Wisdom, share in his power and action as he is the Power of God. The Spirit means that transformation is not merely a hypothetical possibility attained in Jesus; rather, it is a distinct possibility given to each of us.

You may now be asking, what does all of this have to do with the Roman Catholic Church, the church of the Inquisition and the church of Michaelangelo, the church of proud rationalists and of pious, almost superstitious, peasants? Very simple: however you may want to characterize the Church, you have already climbed the steps that lead to it!

How can anyone be a Catholic? By believing in the total transformation of man by God in Jesus Christ.

Man is a social animal. That society must be transformed. God working in our society is what we call the Church. When man's social thought is transformed, we have Church teaching. When man's social actions are transformed, we have Church action.

And we personally are transformed. When God works in us personally, we call that grace. When our thoughts are transformed, we have faith. When our actions are transformed, we have love.

This double transformation is the heart of the Catholic Church. Nothing more mysterious than that. Nothing more weird, arcane, magical, elitist, or arbitrary.

You are staring the Church in the face right now!

6 The Church

"I'd like a soda." A harmless request.

"You're not from around here, are you?"

"Originally, no. I'm from New York."

"I thought so. I'm from New York myself. We always say 'pop' out here, but New Yorkers say 'soda' —sod*er*—so I thought you must be from back there."

Two strangers meeting far from home, establishing contact through community traits ingrained in their speech patterns. Two strangers talking like old friends about subways and mayors, were we there in the great blackout (which one was that?), who is on strike now, and how degenerate 42nd Street is.

It's inescapable. Our backgrounds form and shape us without our being aware of it, mannerisms and prejudices and ways of seeing things made part of us with indelible efficiency. So when we travel here and there, we never feel quite as much at home as when we run into someone who has been tagged much as we have. Instant fellowship from years of social conditioning.

We are skeptical of societies today. Instinctual individualists, we figure we are better off by ourselves. Each one a seeker, each one finding his own solutions or asking his own questions, each one with a personal philosophy that does not have the latent dangers that accompany "mob" thinking or "collective pressures."

We think of communities as *negative* things: communities are established to protect people from each other, to dish out a certain amount to each so that no one will take it all. But they soon seem to act like sponges, soaking everything up, stripping people of any freedoms, digesting constituents with impassive glee.

Yet we can't escape them. We like to talk with people who are like us. Democrats talking with Democrats, Marxists with Marxists, Boy Scouts showing off badges to other Boy Scouts, alumni joining alumni societies, big city people comparing notes, small town people rejoicing that they escaped the big city, nationalities and language-groups getting together to preserve their heritages.

There have always been times (and we just went through one) when communities were viewed with suspicion. "The Establishment" was the enemy. "The Establishment" stood for any kind of external ordering in life. It was attacked as evil, arbitrary, unexplainable, impeding, and tyranical. Wouldn't we all be better living in the woods by ourselves?

But these flutterings of antisocial feeling are very predictable because they are like the occasional flutterings of anti-body feelings that emerge every now and then. For our own human body has been attacked as evil, arbitrary, unexplainable ("Why do I have to be *this* way?"), impeding, and tyrranically demonic. All those deodorants and fancy soaps are evidence of our hate for our bodies as much as they are of our love for them.

Such fits of anti-corporeal and anti-corporate feeling are probably manifestations of our own uneasiness with being limited. We all wish we were unlimited, yet we've only two hands and have to live somewhere with other people. So the truth sometimes hurts—no human bodies, no corporate bodies, then no human beings.

That's the way we are, embodied personally and social-ly.

Basically, we are strangers, seeking to discover and live our oneness—strangers meeting and separating, creating our Woodstocks and making Woodstocks into dreams of unity; strangers designing communities and redesigning them because communities remain so elusive. We hate being strangers, yet we so often are. We form communities because we know that is what we ultimately must be.

And God knows that, too. God, who worked so much in tune with us by taking on our very humanity in Christ, works through the inescapable structures of our human nature. In fact, there is no other way God *could* work with us.

After all, it is not easy for us to deal with God, so full and powerful, so transcendent and intense is he. We shy away. We want to deny. We try doubt. We pervert. We try to be God ourselves—always with the same disastrous results. More pointedly, though, we doubt ourselves, wondering if our dreams are really illusions, questioning ourselves, seeking support, knowing that we can, all by ourselves, maintain only a fragile commitment. If I'm the only one who thinks or believes one way or another, then chances are excellent I'll abandon my belief, yield my thought.

That is why fellowship is so important to us: We can maintain together what we could not individually. Those who have seen UFOs link up with others who have had a similar experience: of course, we saw them, lots of people have! People who belong to a political or philosophical tradition search out others akin to themselves; not only can they share, they can also hold each other up. People with special interests and fields communicate with others in that field, like an intimate group evolving its own language. Our experience ties us with others; our ties with others bolster our experience.

Christian religious faith has experience as its basis. The experience of Jesus Christ by his followers makes the Christian faith possible. This experience is proclaimed by committed men; their commitment attracts others to the same experience. Those who share the insight of Jesus, who experience him, form a religious community so that their experience can be fostered, deepened, and enabled to occur again and again. Take away a community and you've cut off contact with the experience of Jesus. Try making the experience of Jesus into a private, personal affair and it will be close to miraculous if a community does not spring up anyway. That's simply the way we are.

This frightens us because we feel that communities capable of sharing experience are also capable of sharing group illusions. We are afraid of a brainwash. There have been many groups who restrict experience, carefully monitoring it, to insure that members live in a perfectly closed circle of thoughts.

We also feel that communities distort what they set out to maintain. That is, as the experience is passed on from generation to generation, the fire dies down and the insight grows dim. It must be ritualized, rationalized, structured for easy communication—and thereby made cold, lifeless, or irrelevant.

So communities contain liabilities. But what else is new? Everything in life contains liabilities. Those on the "outside" point to an "Eastern Liberal Establishment," while members of the alleged Establishment are only vaguely aware of what others are talking about. Artists view technocrats warily; the feeling is mutual. Governments, universities, geographical regions, fields of discipline, unions, financial interests, even the Boy Scouts —all contain the danger of brainwash. All can distort the human vision. But do we dare wipe these groups out? Only a fool cuts off a finger to shorten a fingernail.

Besides, the deadening that tends to come when an experience is ritualized and passed on from generation to generation seems like another form of the problem of every-dayness—the routine that enshrines important experiences and permits us to return to them at graced moments. A man and woman fall in love. Their love is experienced intensely. They commit themselves to each other and gradually settle into a routine that does not match the initial feeling of love in intensity or fury. Yet, it is only such a routine which permits the experience of love—perhaps on a deeper and more subtle level—to be remembered and to re-occur. If you throw away the good-bye kisses, you've thrown away a lot more than that.

Like general human experience, religious experience is always in danger of being close-headed, of petrifying. The corrective remains the same for all experience: having a diversity of members, maintaining a quest for integrity and honesty, keeping an eye on the larger world and letting it filter in, returning to roots in contemplation and reform. The kinds of rituals, rationales, and structures developed by religious communities permit people to exist in some real, if somewhat removed, contact with the rich experience that called the community together to begin with.

*

God saves the human through the human; God

works with us through our need for community. He has no reason to renounce what he created. Sensual and social, we must encounter God in our senses and in our society. A look at some passages from the Bible, revealing the basic scriptural thrusts about community, can confirm the social ingredient in God's dealings with us.

Among the oldest passages of the Bible, there is a twin emphasis on the power of God and the community of God. A victory chant recorded in the book of Exodus exults: "I will sing to the Lord, for he is gloriously triumphant; horse and chariot he has cast into the sea" (Ex. 15:1). This reflects the thrill of the Jewish people in their escape from slavery in Egypt. Yet one of the major purposes of God's intervention in the Jewish escape was to establish a people, a community, ordered around himself.

The book of Deuteronomy meditates on this theme: "When the Most High assigned the nations their heritage, when he parceled out the descendants of Adam, he set up the boundaries of the peoples after the number of the sons of God; while the Lord's own portion was Jacob, his hereditary share was Israel (that is to say, the Jewish people). He found them in a wilderness, a wasteland of howling desert. He shielded them and cared for them, guarding them as the apple of his eye. As an eagle incites its nestlings forth by hovering over its brood, so he spread his wings to receive them and bore them up on his pinions" (Deut. 32:8-11).

God's concern about forming a community seems to be an indelible strain, present at every step in biblical history. The early call to Abraham begins with this same concern: "I will make of you a great nation, and I will bless you" (Gen. 12:3). The escape from Egypt proceeds right from this promise to Abraham, for the Exodus made the Jewish people into a community and nation. In exchange of God's care and protection, the Jews commit themselves as a group to follow God's covenant: "All that the Lord has said, *we* will heed and do" (Ex. 24:7). The covenant between God and man reads simply: the Jews receive a God, and God receives a people.

The later development of kingship among the Jews (not a uniformly popular development) was made into a religious affirmation of the *community* of Jews. Nathan states to David in a highly influential prophecy: "Your house *and your kingdom* shall endure forever before me; your throne shall stand firm forever" (2 Sam. 7:16). In fact, God's favor toward the king encapsulates his favor for his people. The king and his people were seen as one, the king being influenced by his people, his people being represented by the king.

What happened with the misfortune of the Jews, when the kingdom was not going well? Instead of the community themes diminishing, they increased! More than ever, the Jews, under the inspiration of the greatest prophets, recognized their total reliance on God. God acts in the horrible exile of the Jewish people to Babylon with the same tender power he expressed in Deuteronomy: "Here comes with power the Lord God, who rules by his strong arm; here is his reward with him, his recompense before him. Like a shepherd he feeds his flock; in his arms he gathers the lambs, carrying them in his bosom, leading the ewes with care." (Is. 40:10-11) God's powerful arm shows itself in the care he has for his people.

Ezekiel, who prophesied at the end of the Jewish exile, writes about God's return to the temple in Jerusalem; this is his way of seeing the return of the Jewish people to their land. "The voice said to me: Son of man, this is where my throne shall be, this is where I will set the soles of my feet; here I will dwell among the Israelites forever" (Ez. 43:7). Ezekiel continues to depict the ideal community of God with man in symbolic fashion—the image of the perfect temple in the perfect city. From the experience of God working with the Jewish community, through the experience of purification and suffering in the community's exile, Ezekiel projects the outlines of an ideal kingdom, an ideal city of God, one in which God is intensely joined with his people (Cf. Ez. 36:16ff.).

The great prophets, however, elevated the vision of the Jews beyond their nationalistic horizon. They stressed that, while God dealt with the Jews as his people, his dealings were for all men. All nations someday shall be explicitly part of God's kingdom, God's community. "As the new heavens and the new earth which I will make shall endure before me, says the Lord, so shall your race and your name endure. From one new moon to another, and from one sabbath to another, *all mankind* shall come to worship before me, says the Lord" (Is. 66:22-23).

"This *is* the time of fulfillment. The reign of God is at hand." (Mark 1:15) So Jesus inaugurates his ministry, using the word "reign" or "kingdom" to capture the twin aspect, which we saw present in the oldest Old Testament passages—God's power and community in God. Jewish ideas of kingship, the holy city, the unity of men with God and each other, God's action in human life, man's reliance on God—all these are compressed into the powerful idea of God's *reign*. The kingdom is compared to a feast many times by Jesus (E.g.

Matt. 22:10-12; 25:1-13; Luke 14:15; 15:22-24). Jesus himself hosted feasts that stressed the community of mankind—feasting with those scorned by established Jewish religious society (Luke 5:27-35), and also with his countrymen in the desert when he provided food in an astonishing way (E.g., Mark 6:34-44).

Boldly, Jesus picks twelve men to follow him, to be the object of his special teaching, to prepare other men for his visit (Matt. 9:35-11:1). This embodies in his followers the continuity Jesus felt with his Jewish past: just as "reign" captures so many strands of Jewish thought, so "twelve" recapitulates the twelve tribes of the Jewish nation (Cf. Matt. 19:28). Jesus works with the elements of community brought about in the Jewish people as a backdrop to his own concern with human fellowship.

There is an urgency to the kingdom—it is before his countrymen's eyes, in their midst (Luke 17:21), embedded right in Jesus himself. Trying to escape the political and religious pitfalls of his time (revolutionary insurrectionist, popular wonder-worker, staid religious leader), Jesus consciously directs the attention of the people to himself and his message. The very meaning of the Jewish community is at stake. The true kingdom of God, for which Jewish history was only preparation and image, now is ready to be grasped. The fullness of God's union with man and man's union with man approached with the coming of Jesus.

The followers of Jesus did not miss his point. Through the Spirit that Jesus sent upon his disciples, they formed Christian communities in which Jesus was preached, God praised, and lives changed (Acts 2:42-47). Paul extolled the community which Jesus created by his risen presence: it is Christ's body (1 Cor. 12:12-

31); it is a temple held together by Jesus himself (2 Cor. 6:16; Eph. 2:20-22). John describes the Christian life as incorporation into Jesus: the branches are joined to the vine of Jesus—as each Christian shares in that one, essential, life-giving flow of Jesus' life, each becomes one in him (John 15:1-8).

*

It becomes clear as one reflects on our need for community and God's work among us that, were we to eliminate the factor of community from Jewish and Christian thought, we would be close to missing the whole thing. God, who always deals with us as we are, enters our lives in a social dimension, because the social dimension of our lives is indispensable. God does not save us one by one; he saves us together. This is why an essential part of the sense that Catholics find consists in community. *A community, a church, must be part of full religious experience.* Just as all personal religious experience is structured by some community experience (even Jesus'), so the preservation of a religious breakthrough, such as Jesus', demands society and community.

But the community Jesus brings is complicated, as he was; complicated in its richness, unable to be categorized or analyzed from one perspective alone, condensing divine and human factors in one reality. For this reason, *the community that Jesus brings is, at the same time, a gift and a human product.*

The Church is a gift because it arises at the initiative of God. What pulls Christians together is not merely a feeling of friendship or a need for fellowship. Only the Risen Christ is the basis of the Church—Christ living in his followers through the Holy Spirit. With God's gracious indwelling in the Christian's heart, there comes about the simultaneous indwelling in Christian hearts. Each of us shares in the same reality given to us. Each of us partakes of the same mystery—standing in God's undeserved life. This sharing and partaking is something we cannot demand, establish, or presume.

We have all been influenced by theories of "social contract," which hold that communities are merely the combination of separate individuals who get together by yielding some of their power to an authority so that the authority can protect individuals from each other. To attempt to see the Church in this way, however, will lead us in the wrong direction. Willed by God, shaped by his free action, inaugurated by his revelation, brought to fulfillment by his Son, the Church is a reality that breaks upon us, that calls us together, that nourishes us, that gives so we might receive. In a very real sense, we do not constitute the Church; rather, God constitutes us through his Church. All we receive from God, in one way or another, comes through his Church.

Because the Church is a gift, there is a kind of glory to it. The Church's glory does not lie so much in the cathedrals, the pomp, the golden chalices, or ornate crucifixes. The glory lies in the community itself, existing in a marvelously sweeping sphere, generation begetting generation, snowballing through centuries and epochs and human hearts, with the same recognition of God's presence and Christ's glory magnetizing all joined in Jesus. This is the achievement of the Church, an achievement given by God—its countless unknown saints, the many outstanding ones, the sacramental encounters, the professed creeds, the society of people shaped by a desire for God answered in Jesus Christ.

Even so, the Church cannot be understood merely as a gift: It is also the product of human action. This is so because it is a community of men existing in time and space. For men and with men, the Church is God's way of getting himself into every fabric of human life.

When we talk of the Church, we talk of a community existing in a diversity of times, places, and needs. Indeed, the major breakthrough in the Church occurred with the disciples' recognition that Jesus was savior of all men (not just the Jewish nation), and that all men were called to respond to him in community. Peter professes, "I begin to see how true it is that God shows no partiality. Rather, the man of any nation who fears God and acts uprightly is acceptable to him" (Acts 10:34-35). No restrictions. No genetic requirements or intellectual prerequisites or financial conditions. All men, all flesh (Luke 3:6), all are eligible for sharing the life of the risen Jesus.

So the Church becomes a river, the flowing faith of a community, expanding and flooding all the corners of human life, touching all the areas of human culture, bringing together into one faith the widest diversity of men with their varied philosophies, arts, letters, organizing techniques, music, mind-sets. The river spreads to many banks, picking up different soils and rocks, swishing them along in its flow, in an ever-widening outreach to all men. This is the exact meaning of "catholic"—"for the whole." The Church is for the whole of mankind.

This means we must be as broad-minded as we can in approaching Christian experience. We are often tempted to think of one age of the Church as pristine and pure, with subsequent ages corrupt to one extent or another. But the whole continuum of the Church bears on the meaning of God with us. There is no such thing as "more Church" at one point and "less Church" at another. The salvation of Jesus is offered at every age to all men. We can indicate specially formative eras in the Church's life, in particular the novel and unrepeatable era of the early disciples' preaching. But we will do severe disservice to the diversity of the Church if we cut off era from era and experience from experience—as if the reality of the disciples' early preaching could stop flowing into the next age of the Fathers, then into the age of Cathedrals, of Renaissance, of Reformation, of Enlightenment, or of Vatican II. We may not like some eras as much as others; they may seem less holy, less intelligent, less artistic. But all epochs have borne Christ to us; all epochs have touched men with salvation.

*

Sometime, go to a Catholic church. Not in the afternoon to sit in a quiet church and think. Not to be by yourself with a wisp of incense and the fading stained-glass light wandering on the walls. Not to look at statues or candles or gothic pillars or modern altars.

Go to a Catholic church when Catholics are there, on Sunday morning, or during a weekday worship. Sit down where you can observe, get a wide-angle view of things without being too obvious.

What you will see is people. People no different from anyone else—wiggling, coughing, scratching, correcting children, yawning, chatting, smiling. If you look enough, you will see yourself. For are we not all bound together, parts of each other?

If you continue looking, however, you will not only

see people, you will also see *a people*. A group. A community. For all these different men and women, boys and girls, are pulled together for one reason alone—to worship God in Christ. Some may say hello to a neighbor; others may pray quietly, oblivious of anyone else. Some may appear enthralled and attentive; others may be bored, fending off sleep only by flipping through a leaflet. But all are there for one underlying fellowship.

Christ is the fellowship. The Catholic's life resounds with Christ: present in every dimension, at every point in time, permeating his people, permeating our whole being, Christ ties us into one, making us his body, as intimately joined to us and we are to ourselves.

You will see a people who are instinctively a people, coming to stand together in Christ before the Father, merging together in a holy communion with Christ and with each other. Touched by ordinariness, touched by greatness, this people knows its humanity and knows the graciousness of God whose fingers have pulled into one so many different kinds.

If you have ever dreamed of a united community of man, go to a Catholic church and dream there. For your dream is the Catholic dream, the dream of Christ, enduring through the centuries, enduring in our successes and failures, enduring to give a sense of family to you and to all men.

An early Christian hymn refers to the Church as bread made from grain scattered on the hillside. Indeed, from every hillside, from every people and nation, from every century and culture, a people has been created. We are the grain made into bread; we are also the bread made into Christ's body. We are the Church, God's gift to us so we may find our true, social selves.

7   Church Teaching

Perhaps we've poked through the Bible from time to time, flipping chapters in search of something interesting or inspirational. Perhaps, too, we've put it down again—too obscure, too boring, too many lists of who-begot-whom. We put it down because there seemed better things to do.

Perhaps we've even been introduced to some of the battles over Christian doctrine in a history course. Greeks against Romans, Greeks against Greeks, Protestants against Catholics. Perhaps we've even found these more obscure than the Bible. We never pursued the issue. Again, we had better things to do.

Our fear of Christian teaching seems logical. All these interminable fights seem to have added nothing to human culture or human well-being. Dividing man from man, hair-splitting so refined as to be irrelevant, returning to the same problems in a dozen grotesque disguises—we want none of it. Life should be simpler; religion should be clearer.

But life is never as simple as it seems at first glance. We all run into experiences that we describe as "inexpressible." The event outstrips any words we can find: "I just can't say what I mean." But pretty soon we start finding words to describe the inexpressible, grasping for images and viewpoints. For a very good reason, too: until we find the words, the experience remains almost meaningless to others and we have not digested the experience ourselves. So we compromise. We find words that may not catch the experience completely or even satisfactorily. They may be only signs and indicators of something deeper, tips of the iceberg below, but they are something and they are essential.

The same is true of religion. If Christians do not search for the words to describe the experience of Christ, then that experience dies. So Christians must compromise and find something that works.

In doing so, we inevitably end up "teaching." We pick one word and not another. *This* phrase, *this* emphasis, *this* kind of writing, *this* general tone. Somehow precision is demanded when we deal with words describing an experience. We may not necessarily seek logical precision or grammatical precision; rather, we seek the kind of precision that insures that words will direct our attention in one direction and away from other directions. This is the kind of precision we demand when we're describing something special to someone else—our new house, a great restaurant, someone we've met, a mood we're in.

This precision might mean substituting one image for another, one form of poetry for another, using drama, making arguments, or whatever. It all comes down to the same thing, communicating an experience from one person or group to another person or group. And this, our normal form of "teaching," is the same as Christian "teaching."

Christian teaching is more complicated though, because it has to communicate a very rich experience to a group of people. When this happens, we end up dealing with a *pool* of images and concepts which express a pattern of religious experiences and bring others into that pattern.

A pool. A pool with many currents, many favorite spots, many danger situations, many degrees of depth, many pulls and pushes. As a configuration of genes, which, although determined, can produce many variant and indeterminant effects, the pool of religious teaching can be as limited as one wishes, but still capable of producing remarkable diversity within the same mentality.

So things inevitably get complicated. But should we expect it to be otherwise? Insofar as religion is human, it deals with the experience of humans. So it ends up with the kind of everyday consistent inconsistency that makes up a complex human life. Life is hard, but we cling to it. Love is beautiful, but it always has an element of pain. Decisions are liberating, but we end up chained to them. People are the answer—and the problem.

To expect religion to be a set, geometrical-type of clear propositions with inescapably clear deductions is to expect religion not to be human. If we ever arrive at a consistency that can be grasped simply by reading a book, we have shaved the religous experience down to myopic proportions. Then we would have better things to do.

There is another reason for religion's complexity: it is more than human. If we grant that God can express himself to humans through the experiences of humans, then we have the central Christian paradox of the infinite coming in finite packages, the inexpressible taking on expression. More than ever, we can expect here indeterminacy and variation—richness, complexity, and confusion. Not that God has trouble expressing himself. Rather, God's expression is so overwhelming that no man, no group, no book can keep on top of him.

We should not be surprised, then, if God does communicate himself, he does so in a pool of images and ideas that surround his self-expression. Things will be confusing. But there will be an overall consistency within the flood of images and ideas, throughout the layers of meaning, the ebbs and flows of thought, the different literary expressions and religious concepts.

Usually we can take this kind of wildly consistent situation; on a nonthinking level, we make everyday sense out of God, the world, and personal life through the various threads of religious images. As we move from mood to mood, insight to insight, differing aspects of God's self-communication became heightened and influential. Themes advance; themes recede. It all fits together in the same way we fit together in the different moods, actions, and thoughts that make us up.

But occasionally problems emerge. Revelation demands *concreteness*. With all the diversity of modes of God's self-communication, there still remains the inescapable fact that certain words and ideas are appropriate, and certain ones are not. God can be variously described as Lord, King, Leader, Creator, Savior, Being, Teacher; but he cannot be called dog, demon, slave, chiseler. In the same way, God could have taken on human flesh at any point in history. But the very fact that he appeared twenty centuries ago in Palestine excludes his appearing in Elizabethan England or nineteenth-century Russia.

So we cringe a little bit: God is no longer a totally open ball game. Given the wideness and multiplicity of God's revelation, there still are limits. Not anything goes. There is room for saying, "Yes, this is what we believe. No, this is not what God has revealed in Christ." Perhaps the "yes's" and "no's" have tended to come too quickly at points in history; but when the question is pushed far enough, when one is backed against the wall, then "yes's" and "no's" there simply must be.

*

There appear, then, to be two stages of Church teaching. One stage is the formative one; the other is the critical one. Each stage continues to exist in one way or another throughout the life of the Church.

The formative stage refers to the historical emergence of certain words and ideas to express God and his action. This stage is continued in the absorption of these words and ideas by us who stand in the biblical tradition. The critical stage refers to those key turning points in the Church's existence when the stock of images must be studied and sifted to answer certain pressing questions (e.g., Is Jesus human? What is grace?). This stage is carried on by the Church in its developing reflection and by members of the Church in their image-adjusting which is part and parcel of Christian life.

The Formative Stage

In Christian consciousness, the Bible is the solid effect of the formative stage of God's communication and Church teaching. The Bible is the pool of images and concepts that form the basic framework of Christian thought. This is the "encyclopedia" of assumed terms, of thought and speech patterns, of graphic images, of fundamental arguments, of historical understanding that undergirds the collective thinking of the Christian Church. Just as our own country has a pool of assumed images from its history, institutions, law, commerce, art, and entertainment that structure our collective communication, so the Bible performs the same function in the Church.

The Bible is very effective in its job. So effective, in fact, that modern preachers reproduce, for the most part, in various translated modes, the types—the archetypes—which the Bible offers. Forgiveness will always be tied into the parable of the Prodigal Son. Grace will always find Romans its home. Worship gravitates to the letter to the Hebrews. Creation to Genesis and Isaiah. The Holy Spirit will always straddle John, Acts, and First Corinthians. The foundational stage works!

But how? How does it keep on forming? How does it escape from being a curious document and only that? Because there is a two-way coupling between our everyday life and biblical themes through our prayerful reflection on the Bible. We read something, we have experiences; we match them. We find our experiences enriched by biblical ideas; we find biblical ideas enlivened by our experiences.

All this may seem whimsical or arbitrary. Matching biblical experience with my own experience seems to put the Bible at our mercy, subject to the complex twists of our minds. But this same kind of thing caused the Bible to be written in the first place. For the Bible comes about when people arrive at a penetrating vision of some experience. This vision may be multiple, but it basically consists of viewpoints approaching the same experience. The Jews, for example, escape from Egypt. Fine. Is this Moses' instinct for civil liberties? Or Egyptian weakness? What is the penetrating vision? The biblical viewpoint says: this is the product of God's intervention.

Plagues, staffs, burning bushes, clouds and pillars of fire are all pointing to the same thing—the escape of the Jews is attributable to God alone. Right in the initial experience, we find images shaping the life situation of the Jews, and their life situation shaping the images. Coupling experience and insight. What biblical writers did is the same as we do—only their action is the foundation of ours. In both cases, though, vision and experience are matched. Religious meaning comes at the intersection.

Now, what about this penetrating vision? This, it seems, is as much a product of God's intervention as the event biblical writers are trying to describe. For only when we interpret things from God's point of view do we find religious satisfaction. We can speculate on the why's and wherefore's of some event: this is fun. It is not religious fun, however. It leaves the heart empty, the spirit without hope, the soul still searching. We find nothing crucial or ultimate, nothing saving. But when events are interpreted from God's point of view, showing the action of God and the meaning of his action, then the religious spirit comes alive; it stands up and listens. It doesn't want to miss a note.

Such a satisfying vision cannot be the product of pure human construction. We face a richness that human ingenuity cannot explain, a meaning that outstrips our thinking minds and speaking tongues. We find a satisfaction so complete and convincing that the human heart could not have produced it alone. Everything here reaches beyond the self and comes from beyond the self. We stand in wonder—wonder at what God has done and wonder that we can know and proclaim that.

After all, there is no reason to attribute to God what comes from our own fascinating consciousness. Usually we are not hesitant to claim for ourselves our human products and achievements. Sometimes we even claim more. In this case, we attribute to God what seems come from him because the vision is so penetrating, the view so satisfying. We have the capacity to acknowledge that something beyond our powers causes us to produce beyond our powers at certain key points of human experience.

Inspiration. God raising human consciousness so words come to mean more than words seem able to mean. God raising the intellect of man to see patterns where no patterns seem to be. God raising the mind of man so that words, images, concepts, whole views of history emerge to stare us in the face, leaving us trembling, shaken that our frailty can do what seems impossible.

The penetrating vision of religious experience is like a magnet lining up iron filings; the filings remain the same, but the whole situation, the whole shape is altered. God gives us the power to situate our words, concepts, literary forms, cosmic musings, in such a way that our images exceed themselves and become vehicles of God's self-communication.

So this is the foundational stage of Church teaching: the coupling of experience with description, both at the power of God, yielding religious meaning. Because God's actions represent his universal intention, the expression of his actions are for more than one individual or group. We are not dealing here with private sensations or an esoteric form of mysticism. Rather, we have a cluster of images and concepts that are meant to teach all men.

So the words of one group, through God's power, become formative for all men. Our personal absorption of biblical images does not siphon off a tradition for our personal use so much as it brings us into a tradition and makes us one with it. Indeed, the more we absorb biblical insight, the more we are pulled toward others who share this same insight, becoming part of the community whose mentality is expressed in the Bible.

Biblical communication, like all communication, is a sharing—a sharing, on the one hand, in a common fund of traditions and concepts, and, on the other hand, in God's self-communication to us. In this way, we are humbled, privileged to sift and absorb the flow of God's revelation, responsible for reflecting faithfully on the whole range of the community's reflection. We are waves, receiving what the water brings, being overwhelmed by it, and passing along what we have recieved to another. Overwhelmed and amazed: our amazement stirs wonder, wonder stirs acceptance, acceptance stirs satisfaction, and satisfaction brings transformation of our own minds and the understanding of man.

For throughout the course of our lives, there are peaks of resonance between this worded revelation and our personal experience. We come, through this resonance, to new interpretations of ourselves and our lives. As experience matches revelational experience, we begin to see in a revelational way that life has a purpose, a pattern and destiny; that all is not chance or fate; that the sense we find in our noblest aspirations finds sense in biblical insight.

The Critical Stage

We have our personal experiences and our interpretations of them. But at times we also reflect critically on these. What has really happened in my life? What am I really like? Can I resolve ambiguities enough to make this decision or that one?

In the same way, we reflect critically on the Bible. After we have absorbed enough and gone through the range of biblical expression, questions arise because of the very multiformity of experience. Just as we ask why we are confident one moment and insecure the next, we also ask why God should care about us. Just as we wonder about the tug between good and evil, we wonder whether God's law was presented only to expose the evil of our lives. Just as we wonder why we feel so alone at times, we also wonder why Christ felt abandoned by the Father on the cross.

There is a lot of juggling to everyday life and a lot of juggling in biblical experience. Most of the time we do this instinctively; life has its ups and downs. But sometimes the juggling loses its tempo, one ball flying too far, one hand going too quickly. And sometimes the centrifugal force of a concept grows too great and points of biblical expression expand uncontrolled—and the whole vision is threatened. Paranoia. Scrupulosity. Fixations. However it is said, things get out of hand, questions cannot be suppressed any longer, solutions must be found, the healthy tension must be re-established.

This gives rise to the critical stage of Church teaching whose essential object is to preserve and nourish the richness of the foundational stage. Somehow, with the outgrowth of an unchecked development, the experiences don't match any more. "This is not what I believe. This doesn't feel right. This cannot be the way God acts." When this happens, a resolution of the problem must emerge; the group must act.

The first and best solution, of course, is to have the Bible check itself. If we grasp its images forcefully enough, things can be set straight again. But sometimes this solution is not possible, for the overweening concept, causing the irritation, comes from the biblical text itself. We match biblical text with biblical text, arriving at two impenetrable bubbles, both ready to burst from the internal tension. We sever texts from contexts. We make words into swords. The sword cuts the community. The fullness is lost.

For this, and no other reason, the Church itself, when forced to decide, decides. And not arbitrarily. For the Church in which Christ dwells has a common mind that has been transformed and enlightened. It shares in the foundational stage God has wrought. It has been enlightened not merely by the Bible, but also by the very forces which brought the Bible about—the transcendent action of God within mankind and the enduring action of Jesus, who is Wisdom, in his followers.

Now such Church decisions will be rare. A community can usually live with many different strains in it. But critical situations will occur when the Church either states what it believes or else it falls apart. Like a body, capable of ingesting many substances, the Church can ingest many concepts; but certain substances cause antibodies to form, and certain trends both from within and from outside the body, cause communal antibodies to form.

No Church decision would be appropriate if revelation were not concrete. Without concreteness, it would be possible to have a totally open-ended form of thought and imagination. We could even have contradictions. "This is a nice idea; that one is nice too." But the price for this luxury would be very high—the price of God's self-communication. For a totally open-ended mind really tells us nothing. Really transforms nothing. Even our human experience is not open-ended, the sense we make out of life. We know we are a certain way and not another way; we can do certain things and not other things. If we tried to be totally open-ended, we'd end up in endless circles.

Because of the concreteness of Christianity, critical reflection started, in a rudimentary way, in the New Testament. The Gospels shape traditions about Jesus into a consistent focus attune with the theological and critical reflections of a particular writer living in a particular Christian community. We can see instances where images of Christ are presented to counteract false images. Luke, for example, debunks the notion that Jesus did not have a body at his resurrection (Luke 24:39-43). Matthew answers the charge that Jesus' body was stolen (Matt. 28:12-15). Mark views Jesus as the servant who suffers, while John sees Jesus as the revelation of God's glory in flesh. Each is trying to discipline the images of Jesus to prevent certain distortions.

Even more striking is the New Testament's concern for false doctrine and improper behavior. "For even if we, or an angel from heaven, should preach to you a gospel not in accord with the one we delivered to you, let a curse be upon him!" St. Paul writes (Gal. 1:8). He also says, "The time will come when people will not tolerate sound doctrine, but, following their own desires, will surround themselves with teachers who tickle their ears. They will stop listening to the truth and will wander off to fables" (2 Tim. 4:3-4).The letter to the Hebrews attacks the idea that Jesus is an angel (Hebrews 1:3-4). John talks of "anti-christs"— this very term showing stark contrast between the acceptable and unacceptable. He goes on to say, "You have the anointing that comes from the Holy One, so that all knowledge is yours" (1 John 2:20). James attacks those who separate belief and action (James 2:18-26); Paul refutes those who would enslave the Christian under an ineffective law (Gal. 3:1-3); Paul also rebukes the man living in incest (1 Cor. 5:1-5); Matthew talks of treating the recalcitrant as outcasts (Matt. 18:17); John even envisions holding back the forgiveness of sin (John 20:23).

At times, then, there must be "yes's" and "no's" without any compromise; the image we have of Christ demands some things and excludes others. This critical reflection grew even more intense as questions burned with particular ferocity in later Christian life: Is Jesus an eternal aeon? Is he human? Is he divine? Is God one or many? Is creation good? Is Jesus one or two?

The Church's reaction to these questions was fundamentally instinctive. Enough of the tradition was communicated through generations of believers to produce automatic repulsion to certain errors. Those who worshipped Christ, praying to him, were not about to consider him a mere creature. Those who professed that Jesus was risen from the dead with a glorified body were not able to tolerate positions that debunked human nature or finite existence. If God loved the world, how could anyone call it evil?

But sometimes confusion existed even among committed fellow churchmen. Both worked from the same tradition, each came up with a different and contradictory viewpoint. Here a decision *had* to be made. Some formula had to be worked out that satisfied the evidence of revelation and the religious experiences of men. There followed torturous debate, long arguments, difficult statements. But statements there were. Sometimes the statements seemed like agreements on what the error was; sometimes they seemed only agreements not to disagree.

But these statements emerged from the very viscera of the Church. They affected everyone; they reflected everyone. They reflected the same kinds of tensions found in the foundational revelation of the Church, only on a more precise level. The refrain was simply played on a higher scale.

How did these statements emerge? They came from the life of the Church along the patterns of Church organization. In other words, Church leaders, capsulizing the different vectors of the Church's mentality and composition, worked out critical Church teaching during pressing times. The sense of faith in the laymen and monks exerted itself on spokesmen who were leaders; the leaders worked with the sense of faith received in their local communities to evolve an expression of faith for the whole believing community.

Here the idea of the fidelity and infallibility of the Church comes out. Christ, who is present in his Church, who is Wisdom and Lord, transforms the consciousness of his Church, preserving the transformed consciousness God instilled through his revelation. To imagine the Church betraying the consciousness that God gives it is equivalent to imagining Christ abandoning his Church. Whatever the failings of individual members, whatever the inadequacies of particular schools of thought, the Church remains Christ's body, filled with Christ's mind, communicating and living in the message of Christ.

If bishops or the pope share in this process of communicating the Wisdom, who is Christ, they do so only as necessary aspects of the community Christ is transforming. Once we admit community, we admit as well the necessity of leadership. Once we talk of community actions, we talk necessarily of leaders who execute those actions. Maybe ahead of the community, maybe lagging behind, leaders inevitably arise since the human community must project itself onto leaders for its very endurance.

Leaders, representing in the fullest way the range of the community's membership, have a crucial task in working out solutions to critical problems in Church teaching. Whether the whole Church needs one visible leader to centralize its consciousness and focalize its unity has been debated for centuries. But the idea certainly isn't insane. Of course there has always been suspicion of religious leaders. The Old Testament is very ambivalent about the wisdom of the Jews in asking for a king. (1 Sam. 8) But ambivalent or not, the drive for a central figure in the Old Testament runs throughout: Abraham, Moses, the Judges, even Samuel, who felt horrible about having a king, performed this kind of function in Jewish society. Without some centralizing figure, the centrifugal forces within a community soon grow too great. A rubber band is needed and one human makes an excellent rubber band.

From this point of view, the role of Peter as indicated in Matthew (16:13ff), Luke (22:31—32), and John (21:15-19) along with his persistent mention through the New Testament as a spokesman (or even chief irritant—Gal. 2:11) shows the possibility that such leadership has a place in Christ's Church. But even if we grant the sense that a Catholic makes in having a pope, a pope is still a member of the Church, getting his meaning from it, using his role for it.

*

We have a right to squirm when facing the Bible; we have a right to wince when searching the twistings of Church teaching. Both of them take more work than we feel like giving. But both are crucial to the Church's life. There can be no community without common understanding. We have to have words and ideas that allow us to feel at home, that give us grounds for sharing and communicating, that bind us together. And words are slippery things, concealing and revealing the many layers of human nature.

But we've all done figuring within ourselves. We've all tried to say what our life has meant, to find images in the secret poems of our hearts. And we all have done critical thinking about ourselves, discarding useless fancies and choosing more profitable courses.

So we have within ourselves the kind of actions that the Church does in its process of being God's vehicle of expression. Of course it all is strange. So are we! Of course it all is difficult. But it's the kind of difficulty that alone makes for brilliant human living. Unless we grapple with the words that compose our story, we have no story to tell. Unless we have a story to tell, we run out of meaning, we don't know where we've come from or where we're going. Life comes apart.

Keeping things together is an essential work of Christ, who binds and folds us all into himself. This is why his Church must teach. And this is why the teaching of his Church can, at the same time, help us find him, find each other, and find ourselves. For our story can be his story; when that happens, when our destiny meets up with Christ's, then the convolutions of biblical thought and the contortions of Church teaching have done their job.

8 Church Actions

If we think about it, most of our day is spent expressing ourselves—smiles, frowns, writing, words, gestures, sighs. The way we feel or what we think filters through our many actions, expressing with some accuracy the hidden inside we carry around.

Often our expression is to impress: new, dandy clothes we purchased, or a pen that has a classy name, imprinted envelopes that bear our fine address, a car that says we're flashy or quiet. We arrange and re-arrange our hair, put different colors on our face or different smells under our arms; we sometimes buy snazzy, expensive underwear to impress those blessed enough to know us intimately.

It's a big business, making people seem right and feel right, a business we're only too happy to keep going. For how we express ourselves is tied up with our personalities to such an extent that our self-expression *is* ourselves. If we look dashing, we are dashing. If we look wealthy, comfortable, informal, or belligerent, that's because we *are* those qualities. So we spend hours and dollars creating the kind of person we want to be and appear to be.

But for all we spend, we are investing basically in fads, fashions that will go as fast as they come; so we are not completely tied to these forms of self-expression. Underneath, we know they are trivial even though they seem important.

Every once in a while, however, we come across a brilliantly clear form of expression that lets us express the deepest aspects of ourselves, or lets us touch someone's personality with startling directness. We embody a symbol of ourselves in one form or another which becomes so much a part of ourselves that the symbol is an exquisite code of who we are and what we stand for.

Art is like this. Whether it be jazz or Bach, rock or Broadway; whether ancient urns or modern calligraphy; whether films, buildings, novels or poems—we are taken from ourselves and put in touch with the full force of another person or another idea. In art, the human reaches perfection of expression, communicating to as many or as few as come into contact with the symbol the artist has chosen.

Yet most art is only one-way: we receive, but we do not express back. We are communicated to, but we do not get a chance to communicate. So we seek forms of expression that are two-way, and we find these very rare treats. The actors in a play make magic between themselves through the playwright's skill. Collaborators in a complex technological feat erect a powerful image of their labor and dreams. We remember, perhaps, a half-dozen conversations when our words wove so smoothly with our thoughts and with the words of another, when two thoughts touched each other in trusting honesty. And we recall, perhaps, the occasions when our bodies became symbols of love with another and two became one.

Expression lies at the heart of Catholic sacraments, for these sacraments are acts that fulfill a very complicated communication between Christ and his followers. These actions contain three essential components:

1) They are *external*. We embodied people like bodily things. For all the importance we attribute to the internal states of our minds and hearts, these internal states naturally spring to external expression. Our minds form words; we can't get along without words. Our decisions emerge into action; our intentions are real when we act on them. This is why all of us are instinctively suspicious of wordless ideas ("Just what's he talking about?") and actless intentions ("Does he really believe that?"). Even the platonic lover, after all, writes poems to the beloved. We like external things.

2) They are *dramatic*. We all love some kind of drama, something that jars us out of the ordinary and shakes us enough so that we look up. Even when we narrate events in our lives, we dramatize, moving our hands, screwing our faces into different poses, altering our accents to mimic different parts of the remembered events. Drama makes things important, adds a dose of emphasis, highlights the unusual hidden in the usual.

3) They are *stylized*. We are not fans of stylized behavior and events, usually; but at certain points, we demand that an expression be stylized. When we are trying to capture something decisive with a past or a tradition, we demand formulas and rituals to heighten our sense of contact with the past or tradition. We want to eliminate arbitrariness, the feeling that what is being done is off-the-cuff. Weddings, graduations, trials, inaugurations—these and other events are usually stylized to satisfy our need for belonging in a context larger than the span of our life.

When we talk of Church actions, we are talking about ritual expression that comes from the heart of the Church as Christ's community. We exclude the actions of particular churchmen, we exclude even the actions of members of the Church. Church actions refer to actions of the Church as Church: structured events that flow from the Church and express what the Church is all about.

Now, the Church is a very peculiar society. It is a fellowship that joins man to man in Jesus Christ. God initiates the Church; Christ constitutes it; the Spirit gives it life. Yet the Church remains remarkably human. Because of this complex origin, divine and human, the Church expresses itself in symbol—in acts and signs that provide communication between God and man. As we seek peak moments of expression in which we express ourselves and touch the heart of another, so the symbols of the Church enable it to express the human reality of its members and encounter the mystery of God in Christ.

What do symbols do? They are external events, words, or deeds, that indicate and embody an underlying meaning. The reality of God's revelation, of Christ's Lordship and presence, simply cannot be expressed by arbitrary words or off-the-cuff gestures. Too much is at stake. Arbitrary words and gestures may miss more than they hit. So symbols emerge—events, deeds, and words which communicate and compress a profound and meaningful reality.

Symbols not only communicate the presence and meaning of God; they also communicate with the nature of man, for these symbols emerge from the common forms of human life, the needs of our nature, the key points of our lives. In one symbol, then, God and man are re-expressed to each other. Symbols allow a meeting point.

Jesus himself is, of course, the prime Christian symbol, for he is the exact meeting point between God and man. He symbolizes God to us, showing us the inner nature of God; and he symbolizes man to God, living a life of total dedication to his Father.

But our need for symbols does not vanish with the glorification of Christ. For this does not abolish our bodily existence; we still remain men, needing to see things, wanting to be part of the drama. So Jesus in his Lordship continues to work in and through his Church, using the actions of the Church—the actions of Christian men together—to continue the communication between God and man.

Naturally, then, these symbols pull in two directions. They pull toward our human existence, for they emerge from our human life—water, oil, bread, wine, reconciliation, married love, and community functions. They also pull toward Jesus, for through these symbols Jesus continues to bring the assurance of his presence and power, to effect his grace. Right where these two directions come together lies worship—the presence of man to God and the revelation of God to man. These symbols form the basis of Church action—the worship in which God and man stand in ecstasy toward each other. Communication.

The worship-actions of the Church are located at key points in human and community experience. Birth, maturity, the taking of ministry, marriage, the experience of moral and physical failure, the need for constant nourishment—these are the key points that touch our personal lives and constitute the Church's life. Any society must face up to central moments like these. All societies with extensive scope deal with issues like birth, the age of plurality, elected office, marriage rites, courts, hospitals, economy. When symbols entwine with these key points in Church worship we end up with the sacraments, with baptism, confirmation, holy orders, penance, anointing the sick, matrimony, and communion. God seizes these key points of life to instill a transformation of human life which we call salvation.

*

First of all, there are sacraments of Church structure. Every society has ways of marking off the function and social recognition of its members. Every society deals with membership, investiture, and leadership. Even in societies that try to down-play these structural forms, there emerges an instinctive awareness of those who join, of those who are established, and of those who take responsibility. Most mature societies have recognized ways of marking off these forms and functions in the community. The Church marks off these forms and functions through the sacraments of baptism, confirmation, and holy orders.

Baptism is the sacrament that extends membership in the Church. It is the most extensive sacrament, using the most extensive symbol—water—to show the availability of membership to all men. Through baptism, a person is inserted into the fundamental worship of Jesus Christ. He shares in the death and resurrection of Jesus; he is taken up into Jesus' dying and rising. St. Paul argues this most forcefully. "Are you not aware that we who were baptized in Christ Jesus were baptized into his death? Through baptism into his death we were buried with him, so that, just as Christ was raised from the dead by the glory of the Father, we too might live a new life. If we have been united with him through likeness to his death, so shall we be through a like resurrection." (Rom. 6:3-5)

Because baptism is the most extensive sacrament, the expectations for its reception are the most general: faith in Jesus Christ. This faith may be expressed on different levels. The basic level, however, is one of acceptance, the willingness to accept salvation and insertion into Jesus. We are receivers; God is the giver, through Christ. The willingness to receive, to place no obstacles, is the elemental disposition for receiving this sacrament. This is why there is no hesitation in baptizing infants. The undisputable time for receiving is childhood. Just think of all that children receive from their parents: food, clothing, sex, race, ways of thinking and speaking, values. Along with all of these, should not a child also receive the Lord Jesus? If Christ has had such a decisive impact on the life of parents, should this impact be restricted and withheld from the child? By no means. Children belong to God's kingdom, too. If the parents, then, have faith and intend to pass this faith on to their children, then "let the children come." (Matt. 20:14) This receptive attitude of baptism is part of what a Catholic means by grace: God's loving us even before we can love him fully.

The water used in baptism carries human connotations of cleanness, destruction, and life-sustaining qualities. These human connotations are linked with biblical connotations to form a complex human-Christian meaning. So Naaman (the foreigner!—cf. Lk. 4:27) comes to Elisha to be washed clean from his leprosy (2 Kings 5:1-15). The flood purges the earth of wickededness in the story of Noah (Gen. 6, esp. verses 5-7). And Moses taps the rock in the desert by which water is given to the thirsting Jews (Ex. 17:1-7). These images are themselves crystallized in the crossing of the sea by the Jews in their escape from Egypt (Ex. 14:10-31).

People who receive baptism are crossing a gulf that sep-
arates sin, slavery and death from holiness, freedom
and life.

Crossing a chasm is needed because of our need
for salvation. There must be a "past" of sin in all of us;
this "past" must be destroyed. In fact, the levels of sin
that must be destroyed are complex. Even *before* any
personal sin on our part, we are en-webbed in sin. Indeed, this webbing extends to the full range of personal
and historical human existence. "Therefore, just as
through one man sin entered the world and with sin
death, death thus coming to all men inasmuch as all
sinned. . ." (Rom. 5:12). We need no great powers of ob-
servation to discern the envy, greed, anger, and lust
that come built-in to our human nature. Nor do we
need tremendous study to acknowledge that invariably
everyone will put that envy, greed, anger, and lust to
work; once the capacity to actualize these tendencies
occurs, they will be actualized. For this reason, all men
exist with a "past" of sin, by their very birth. The destructive qualities of the water-symbolism point to the
destructive work of Christ in facing sin and destroying
sin.

The life-giving qualities of water symbolize, in
turn, the newness won for men in the risen glory of
Christ. Baptism is viewed as new birth, a regeneration,
a clean break with the "past" and new dynamism for
the future. The newness comes precisely with the insertion of the baptized into the very act of Christ's dying
and rising. We are reprogrammed and restructured according to the form of Christ's saving act. We are given
powers to act in Christ, sharing his priesthood, prophecy, and kingship. We are structured and patterned into

him. This is the basis of our transformed Christian existence.

This basis is extended and intensified in confirmation. Confirmation is the finishing mark of baptism. Whereas in baptism we receive the newness of Christ in an initiating way, in confirmation we receive the fullness and maturity of Christ's newness in finalizing way. As the salvation won by Christ was finalized in the Spirit which he sends on his Church, so the salvation given us in baptism is finalized in the intensification of the Spirit given with confirmation.

Such a need for finalizing and fullness emerges from the transition people undergo upon entering a community. At one point, they are admitted, but they are basically *receivers*. Their initial time is spent receiving the properties of their new-found society. At some point, however, the new member attains a recognition as "established"—he is a giver, rather than only a receiver. He can take responsibility to extend what he has received to others outside the community. There is an enthusiasm, a missionary slant, a witness-factor that was only latent at the beginning. The book of Acts reads: "When the apostles in Jerusalem heard that Samaria had accepted the word of God, they sent Peter and John to them. The two went down to these people and prayed that they might receive the Holy Spirit. It had not as yet come down upon any of them since they had only been baptized in the name of the Lord Jesus. The pair upon arriving imposed hands on them and they received the Holy Spirit" (Acts 8:14-17).

Confirmation is a deeper molding into the pattern already established in baptism. The signs of this sacrament are oil and the imposition of hands. Oil symbolizes the strength and capacity for readiness that a Christian receives with confirmation. Oil was widely used as a muscle lubricant in ancient times. The very name of Christ means "Anointed," since the pouring of oil designated one chosen by God for a task. The imposition of hands indicates the reception of fullness; for every sacrament is a gift.

Baptism is intensified even further with the reception of holy orders. This is the assumption of service and leadership for the good of the whole Church. Here the pattern of Christ is so deepened that those receiving holy orders take upon themselves, in Christ, the charge of maintaining the worship and teaching of the Church. What is received in baptism, participation in the death and resurrection of Jesus, now is exercised in a most intense and public way.

Church leaders exercise the leadership of the *Church*. It is not so much their own insight, holiness, or managerial skill that accounts for their leadership; rather, what subsists in the Church comes to conscious and public exercise in the leaders, much as a national leader exercises the reality of a nation. Leadership itself is a gift, flowing from the serving witness of Jesus, with duties and responsibilities given to his Apostles so they might serve all of Jesus' followers.

For this reason, ordination is given by bishops—those successors of the Apostles—through the imposition of hands. The minister receives from Christ through the bishop the charge and the power to serve the Church in a total and exclusive way. Whether deacon, priest, or bishop, those in holy orders are to be dedicated leaders through their dedicated service. (Cf. 2 Tim. 1:6)

Since these sacraments, which structure the social

fabric of the Church, are shares in the eternal, worshipping reality of Christ, they are not repeatable. Christ's pattern is formed in us with the fullness of his eternal worship in varying degrees; but that pattern is unerasable just as Christ's worship is unerasable.

*

If Christ is transforming mankind through his presence in the Church, then there is no way that marriage can be excluded from this transformation. For there is no more decisive aspect of human life, in terms of human growth and the future of the race, than marriage. Marriage reaches into every element of life: our intimate sexual lives, the give and take of committed persons, the subtle process of education, the quality of a nation. Marriage is the key to so much of what we call life.

Christ's saving activity extends in and through marriages which are done in his name. Marriage is a sacrament, too. This human basic is taken over by God and made to symbolize and bring about the profound presence and saving activity of the Lord. Through marriage, new members are born to the Church, the values of Christian life are inculcated, lives become entwined in one meaning, the secular is made most graphically sacred.

To say that marriage is a sacrament is to say that through the married love of man and woman, Christ becomes present and his saving activity occurs in the midst of human life. The man and woman bind themselves into one not merely with their own commitment and love—all human marriage should be that—more, they bind themselves with the very commitment and love and will of Jesus Christ. This is the dignity of those born in the Lord: to act with the power of Christ. Men and women who marry in Christ are acting with his power to become one in love and life. St. Paul says, "Husbands love your wives, as Christ loved the Church. He gave himself up for her . . . Husbands should love their wives as they do their own bodies. He who loves his wife loves himself. Observe that no one ever hates his own flesh: no, he nourishes it and takes care of it as Christ cares for the church—for we are members of his body" (Eph. 5:25-30). Paul's logic is clear. As Christ becomes one with his body, the Church, husbands become one with their wives. With the same force, will, dedication, and power by which Christ is joined to the Church, the married couple is joined together.

This is why all of married life is sacred. It is sacramental. It is a life of holiness, in which the worship of Christ is threaded through the whole fabric of life. The very worldliness that we associate with marriage is transformed into the very sacredness we associate with Christ's presence to God and to man.

So the married couple represent not only themselves; they represent the Church as well. They are the Christian community extending the holiness of God into the finest parts of human existence. This is their sacred charge and vocation. Every act of love, every bit of generous sacrifice, every struggle to understand, every attempt to raise the children and bring them into Christ—all of this is sacramental, all is worship. No wonder divorce is intolerable to Catholics. For all the compassion extended to those in broken marriages, at the same time the Church's eyes are kept firmly rooted in the exaltedness of marriage in the Lord.

Take away the sacramentality of marriage, and

one has taken away one of the strongest pillars of the Church. Without marriage, it cannot survive. The community is stilted and stunted. With marriage, however, we have an effective and profound symbol of Christ's transforming reality.

*

Failure has always been a problem in human life. Why all this potential should go haywire, why the arrow should miss its target, why the human seeking for good should stumble along the way—these questions are wrapped in the mystery that we call human nature as we experience it. Whatever insight we can glean from scripture and the human sciences, we are forced to discount attempts to blame error on the creator, on fate or chance, on genes and environment, or on any other factor aside from the human will itself. For all the conditioning factors that play upon the will, ultimately it is the will, simple human choosing, that is the root of moral failure.

That Christians fail is equally unexplainable, but equally obvious. For all that God does to and for us, we are still radically free and radically able to act in accord with God's revelation and grace, or to act against his revelation and grace. Transformation is, after all, a process. The powers of transformation are present with Christ's saving activity, but the extension and working of those powers is a slow and gradual thing. Paradoxically, we must become what we are! This very becoming is latent with the possibility of not-becoming, of failure.

Christ, who always offered the greatest ideals to his followers, was also realistic enough to recognize failure. The seed sown does not invariably produce the best yield (Mark 4:1-9). The field that is sown contains weeds as well as grain (Matt. 13:24-30). And the field capable of producing useful grain and useless weeds is at the same time his community and the individual within the community.

Failure does not spell the end, however. Transformation is a process capable of coming to fullness through correction. If judgment is an inescapable part of following Christ (John 3:18-21), mercy is also an inescapable part of God's attitude toward us (John 8:1-11). Thus, within the general conversion toward Christ, there is room for subsidiary reconversions, turning again to the God we once accepted and the God who accepted us and gave us his life.

In the face of Christian failure, three possibilities are possible: (1) we can deny the failure, in which case we are suffering from illusions or radical self-deception; (2) we can deny the ideals by which we should live by any tenuous process of rationalization; (3) we can admit our failings in the face of ideals.

Only the third possibility is open, really, for a Christian. And it is precisely this possibility that has been exercised by the Church from its beginning: the frank admission of fault; the humble return to God, like the prodigal son (Luke 15:11-31); the admission that ideals have been knowingly and needlessly violated.

The failure has also been seen to lie in three directions. The first direction is toward oneself. Sin is self-failure. What we hold dear and valued we have not followed. Our very ideals have been compromised. Our self-image is smashed. The second direction is toward God. We have refused to answer God's call for dedication and commitment. Having set up another god before him (the god of our self-will and self-rule), we have cast him aside. He is no longer treated as the transcendent Lord of all life. Instead, we have tried to become Lord ourselves. Finally, the third direction is toward the community of believers who share Christ's life. The body of Christ is to reflect the holiness of Christ, being spotless and pure (Eph. 5:26-27). We have robbed the body of the holiness that belongs to her. We have offended our fellow-man (even in the most secret of sins!) and detracted from the community in which he lives (Cf. 1 Cor. 12:26).

Catholicism, which sees penance as a constant factor in Christian life, recognizes the need for clear acts of penance and reconversion in serious sin. Serious sin fundamentally contradicts the life and values that Christ has given us. It is a decision to abandon God. It leaves us dead to Christ's Spirit, which we have thrown out. The remedy for serious sin cannot be simply a rethinking on our part, a cerebral act, penetrating though that may be. It must be a public act of making peace with oneself, one's God, and one's community. Unless it is public, we have not taken the public nature of sin into account. Nor are we quite so sure of the sincerity and seriousness of our intentions. Nor can we be fully assured of peace and reconciliation.

For this reason various forms of public penance and confession have existed throughout the whole history of the Church. The present form practiced in Catholicism, confession of sin to a priest, arose from the need of a more practical and less severe (though no less serious) method of dealing with sin. The priest represents the community of believers and the Lord who extend reconciliation to anyone who sincerely repents of

sin and who assure forgiveness in a very direct and
human way. There can be no doubt that the community
does have a say in the moral conduct of its members
(Cf. Matt. 18:15-18; John 20:22-23; 1 Cor 5:1-5). That
the community exercise this function with discretion,
privacy, and fraternal assistance through its ministers is
certainly a plausible and natural way of dealing with
failure. Whatever reluctance we have to confessing, it
remains fairly clear that unless we deal with our failures concretely and directly, it is nearly impossible to
cooperate with the transformation God is working in us
through Christ.

Physical failure and death are crucial points in
both human life and community life. A community that
does not deal with sickness and death has little maturity
and little realism. The Church, as Christ's community,
continues his own concern for the sick and the dead
through its sacraments. The sacrament of sickness is
that of anointing.

James writes of the ministry of aiding the sick in
his epistle: "Is there anyone sick among you? He
should ask for the presbyters of the Church. They in
turn are to pray over him, anointing him with oil in the
Name of the Lord" (James 5:13-14; cf. Mark 6:13).
The medicinal and strengthening qualities of oil, as em-
ployed in early medicine, symbolize the medicinal and
strengthening qualities of Jesus' risen life. The prayer
and the sacrament of the sick intercede before God with
Christ's very victory over death, and therefore over the
factors of human weakness.

Sacramental care for the ill allows a transfer between the sick and the Church vital for both. It keeps
the Church in close touch with sickness and death, forc-
ing an awareness of the crises of human life at the heart

of man's dilemma. Only in this way can the utter necessity for salvation be acutely felt. It also keeps the sick aware of the reality of the Church, the union of God and men in Christ which can never be ripped away through sickness or death. That union, in fact, forms the eternal basis of Christian life.

That sickness and death can become acts of worship runs very close to the kind of renewal possible for mankind in Christ. Here, what is symbolized and structured in baptism takes on a sharpness and starkness that leaves the human trembling. Our death is passage into God; we die with Christ—we pass over to God. Sickness, as the anticipation of death, shares also in this passage of Christ from death and defeat to life and fullness. "I wish to know Christ and the power flowing from his resurrection; likewise to know how to share in his sufferings by being formed into the pattern of his death. Thus do I hope that I may arrive at resurrection from the dead" (Phil. 3:10-11).

*

All these worshipful actions, in which an earthly symbol is used by Christ in his Church to bring about union and contact with his people, have their culmination in the act of worship *par excellence*, the Christian eucharist. It is in the eucharist that the Church says what it most is; it is here that God's union with man in Christ is most dramatically manifest.

The eucharist is an action in which man gives thanks to God for what God has done. The word "eucharist" derives from the Greek word for giving thanks. Such thanksgiving is no luxury for a Christian or for any believer; it is the essence of his attitude toward God.

Thanks acknowledges God as truly God, the transcendent one who has stooped to love us, who permits our very being, who renews our very being. Thanks says that God is the heart of all, the beginning and the end, the one essential dividing line between what is real and what is illusion. To take God precisely as our ultimate constitutes belief. To reject God as our ultimate constitutes idolatry and unbelief. If one believes, then, one gives thanks.

Such giving thanks pulls together other basic strands of religious life, such as obedience and request. It is not arbitrary that the letter to the Hebrews, which so demarcates Jesus as worshipper, also pinpoints his life and ministry as one of obedience (Hebrews 10:4-10). Jesus can be summed up as the one who comes to do God's will. As worshipper and as obedient Son, Jesus is intercessor: he makes requests on our behalf. "Therefore he is always able to save those who approach God through him, since he forever lives to make intercession for them" (Hebrews 7:25). For request, too, is acknowledgment of God's ultimate generosity and our essential dependence on him.

Jesus is, thus, the central priest and fundamental worshipper of God. His thanks, which is God's gift to us, also is the ultimate thanks that we can give God. To worship means to worship in Jesus. To worship means giving Jesus' thanks, obedience, and intercession is our own thanks, obedience, and intercession. As every sacrament is insertion into Christ, the eucharist inserts us into Christ as he stands before God. Christ, man united with God, God united with man, stands as the touching point between God and mankind.

The gift of sharing in Christ's worship was given at the Last Supper when Christ gave his body—broken for us—to his apostles, and his blood—shed for us—to his followers. By this Christ is saying, "My death is your death; my resurrection is your resurrection." The worship of Jesus' obedient death now becomes extended to Jesus' followers, those who share in Jesus' life.

The insertion into Christ is real. We are not dealing here with symbolism in any loose or arbitrary way. The Christian really shares in the death and resurrection of Christ. He really shares in Christ's worship. He does this through the presence of Christ in his followers. Christ lives in us; he lives united to us. We are not mimicking; nor are we being nostalgic.

The union of the Christian with Christ is symbolized in the intense union of food, eaten, taken into us, becoming part of us. Here, as in all the sacraments, the symbolism is strong: bringing about what is symbolized. The union of Christ with his people is brought about by the eating of food radically identified with him. "This is my body; this is my blood." In his risen power, Christ is identified with the bread and wine as he is with his own body. As through his body, Christ is present, so through the bread and wine identified with him, Christ is present. This is why Catholics regard it almost as a mistake to call the sacred bread and wine, bread and wine; it functions like bread and wine, but it *is* the reality of Christ.

In the bread and wine, we give thanks to God through Christ. We become mysteriously and really united to Christ as worshipper. We achieve the most intimate expression of our union with him. Christ's union, in his Church, in his scriptures, in all the sacraments, shows forth most truly in the eucharistic bread and wine at the heart of the Church's worship in him.

The intense union with Christ, which the eucharist

brings about, also intensifies the union brought about, in Christ, between one believer and another. Here one life runs through the body of Christians. Here one union defines and constitutes the Christian community. Here, the Lord, joined to each, joins each to each in his very body: "Is not the cup of blessing we bless a sharing in the blood of Christ? And is not the bread we break a sharing in the body of Christ? Because the loaf of bread is one, we, many though we are, are one body, for we all partake of the one loaf" (1 Cor. 10:16-17).

This union with Christ happens through the glory existing in Christ as he is Lord of the Church and Lord of Creation. The transcendence of God, his absolute power and love, is received by Christ and exercised by Christ. This is why Christ rebukes those who reject the mystery of the eucharist with the words, "Does this shake your faith? . . . What, then, if you were to see the Son of Man ascend to where he was before?" (John 6:62) Given the power of the resurrection, then even the ability to be present to his people as their food and drink is possible. And, through the food that Christ becomes for us, he gives us the power of resurrection in him: "If anyone eats this bread, he shall live forever" (John 6:51).

*

Getting along without symbols is impossible. Without symbols, we cannot understand ourselves, nor can we express ourselves. Without self understanding and self-expression, the project known as human nature collapses.

Without symbols, we cannot know God either. For how would God express himself to us? There would be no way for us to grasp him, no handle to take hold of. What is not symbolized to us does not exist for us.

We reach for symbols and gestures at every point in our life—the words that clothe the vaguest notions of our minds, the violent gestures that punctuate our feelings, the chosen gifts that say what we mean. God, too, reaches for symbols in reaching for us. With the same brilliance used when encoding himself in our flesh, he continues to touch us through the basic signs and needs and actions of our lives.

The more penetrating the symbol, the more impact in communication. That is why God uses symbols that surround our daily existence, that hinge our personal and social lives, to communicate his surrounding care and his pointed love. We, likewise, use these symbols to express our own hearts to him, our willingness to be taken over by him, our daring to love in his name, our self-offering to him, our acknowledgment of guilt and repentance, our reliance on his help, our desire to serve him more fully.

The symbols then become an interface between God and us, the permeable membrane that brings the power of God into our lives and brings our lives into God's powerful kingdom. At these symbol-filled junctures, our lives take on God's meaning and power, leaving aside the self-defeating insecurity that makes us desperate, taking on the pattern of Christ's eternal trust that makes us men of peace.

These symbols bring transformation. At the juncture of God's expression and our expression comes change, the use of our lives to renew our lives, the things of our lives becoming fulcrums of new life.

We are hopelessly communicators, searchers, symbolizers, worshippers. We know we cannot stand alone.

We know we must reach out. We know our reaching has no limits. We know we need an answer.

Part of that answer consists in God's reaching out, wanting to make something happen in us, calling us to be in him, where we should have always been. Like fine stitching, the sacraments have threaded our personal lives and the generations of the Church together; threaded together, they have been bound to God, for no other binding could satisfy him or us.

9 Grace

Twenty years old. Sunshine fills the world. Haven't seen a cloud for a year or so, and weather looks fine ahead.

Young, healthy, intelligent enough, acceptably good-looking, putting together the pieces of life into a picture that says our life looks like it's going to be a success. Perhaps we're off to college: we're going into law, or business, or humanities, or science. Perhaps we're bypassing college, apprenticing ourselves in one of the many trades. Either way, life is going our way. We can smell the lawn freshly cut on Saturday mornings outside our future house. We hear eggs and bacon crackling in the frying pan. We hear the sounds of our children, the labors of our spouse, the music subconsciously emphasizing the goals sought and won.

Twenty years old. We've perhaps been there. We're perhaps heading there now. A bundle of energy waiting to strike, anxious to make the world come alive under the skill of our delicate but powerful hands.

So we choose. We put the energy to work. We go places, we study things, meet the right people, get up and clean up after our mistakes, buzz along with dreamlike rapidity until we're soon twenty-one, thirty-one, fifty-one. We choose; we come about. We work; we get our dreams. Horatio Alger come alive! Keeping our nose to the grindstone has formed a face that others recognize as successful; even we do, from time to time. We've made it—the transition, the parabola of a life shot from possibility to accomplishment.

For all the aggressive enthusiasm, however, the transition from possibility to accomplishment seems as much a product of luck as of hard work. All that marvelous talent does not come from any planning or choice: it is given with the package we call ourselves. The many components we pick up from family and friends need not be to our advantage; we could have been poor, our parents could have died when we were young, they could have misshaped our personalities hopelessly.

The dreams we have flow from our experiences in life: these could have been destructive experiences, tearing apart every shred of security we have, leading us to expect failure, to give up before we start, to accept things as they come along without any energy on our part.

A dozen things could have dismembered our plans: war, sickness, an economic depression, mental instability, mistakes, drugs, changing work opportunities, loss of interest, alcohol, a changing family situation, other offers we couldn't refuse, opposition from others opposing our plans. The whole edifice could have come down at any time for any number of reasons; yet it didn't.

So we call it luck, perhaps. Luck that we have been able to work with what we have to make a few hopes come true, to carry out some plans. Luck that everything that could have gone wrong did not go wrong. Luck that our capacities were able to amount to something instead of being wasted.

Yet this is a luck that we take for granted. For when we think of luck, we think of it being both good and bad. Things go our way; things do not. Somehow, though, when it comes to the business of life, we expect things to go our way. We *presume* that plans will work out. We presume that this bundle of talent and charm we pamper in the mirror every morning will have a talented and charming life.

Even when bad luck besets us, when plagued with the greatest of trials, we operate on an expectation of good luck. The biblical Job may say that the Lord gives and takes away (Job 1:20), but we are not so placid. Things should have gone our way, we think; this hardship should not have come; this life should not amount to a trivial jest. When we experience bad luck, we experience it with bitterness and disappointment. We deserve better.

Or do we? Somewhere in the age span between the possibilities of 20 and the actualities of 40, there sneaks across our minds the unnerving hint that we really *deserve*, strictly speaking, nothing. The whole show is being produced for us. The whole thing is handed to us. Nothing has to be; certainly, the universe can whirl around without any of us. There is no essential reason for me to have my kind of looks, my mental ability, my energy, my humor, my opportunities. Yet here it is: trickling out of nowhere, I stand as a compromise of many chances, assuming what I have received, presuming what I do and will receive.

Think about the chances involved in a life. We live in one part of the world, one part of the city, attending one school and not another. In this one school, we find ourselves influenced by one set of friends, or one particular teacher, or engrossed in one field of interest and not another. The twig is bent. How much have *we* bent it? The boy who likes to collect and mount insects becomes the scientist; the girl who likes to sing ends up playing the piano. One person takes up a dissolute life and finds himself content to be widely experienced and not naive; another person leads a quiet life and is content with his quiet family, in a quiet house, on a quiet street, in a quiet town.

Patterns emerge in our life that we cannot explain, that we do not deserve. We become successful. We find the right husband or wife. Just the perfect job! We become the intricate weave from the ball of wool. We become what we are, almost in spite of ourselves. Sure, we work hard, diligent application over many years, noses to the grindstone. But the reason we work hard, where we get our inexhaustible energy, why we think success is even important: these are gifts, these, too, ae undeserved.

For all the chance in life, for all the disappointment, for all that we do not deserve, we make presumptions on life because our guts tell us that there is a point to living. As soon as we wonder over the classical question, "Why is there something rather than nothing," we begin to realize that there must be some point to being. We do not feel that we won the flip of an unbiased coin. We feel, rather, that we were chosen, that there is purpose, that life is not as arbitrary as it could be.

Why is there something rather than nothing? Why are things the way they are? Why am I? Far more than endless hours of philosophical discussion, these questions bring us to the utmost realization of the giftedness of our whole existence, the intractable feeling that we are objects of underserved attention. Unexplainably, it seems, reality is taking care of us.

When we have arrived at this kind of feeling and attitude, we have arrived at the primal experience necessary for understanding grace. If we think we can account for everything, that we are totally responsible agents, that we deserve everything we have, then grace will forever remain a nonsense idea. But if we have ever wondered "Why me?," then we are only a breath away from appreciating what grace means.

*

Grace is the offer and reception of love when love is not deserved. The word "love" need not mean deep emotional feeling or erotic pangs; it may simply mean "to be chosen—to be given attention." When the religious man thinks of grace, he has in mind a multi-layered relationship in which a generous God extends his love to those who cannot claim it, nor earn it, nor ever deserve it.

Just being created is an act of grace. No one demands to be created; no one can earn it. It is a result of God's generous and originative power in as strict a sense as we can imagine. For God has nothing to gain in his creation for himself; as God, he exists in unrestricted fullness. There is nothing to be "filled in" or "perfected" in him. So there is no motive for creation except the generous sharing of existence. God's gain is the gain of his creation. This accounts, at once, for why we feel so frail and so secure in our life.

Yet being created is only the first level of grace. Grace further means being chosen by God as friends, even though we do not deserve the relationship of friendship. We do not deserve this relationship with God, not merely because God's reality exceeds our own in every dimension, but also because our own existence has been torn apart by the destructive decisions we have made to live outside of and against God.

Indeed, we have made the very existence that God has given us into an opportunity for rupturing the basis of a relationship with him. Because we are given our existence, we feel insecure, humbled, finite. This insecurity, humility, and finiteness can become the occasion for either resentment or accepting our created status. When we accept our created status, we find security in our creator; we no longer survey creation as if we were omnipotent, we accept our limitations and find fulfillment in what we are. But when we resent our created status, instead of acknowledging a creator, we strive to ground our own security, surveying creation as if we were total masters and capable of all; we open ourselves up to the prospect of endless unfulfillment. For we seek what is unreal. We must pay an impossibly high bill with a deficit of cash. We die playing God.

That mankind has resented its created status seems abundantly clear. That this has lead to the rupturing of our relationship with God is inevitable. We have lost sight of the innate desires of our own hearts for God; we have made ourselves our only desire, causing the harmony of our existence to go awry much like playing a record whose center hole is disfigured. Becoming our own ends, we become laws for ourselves. We define life for ourselves: murder emerges. We define truth on our terms: lies and self-deception. We define love and give birth to hate. We define justice from our viewpoint: war, robbery, poverty, and exploitation result.

It is not so much that we do not know life, truth, love, or justice. We know them. But we distort them. We compulsively distort and blur the very values we know we need. We do this because we want to give ourselves our own values and not seek them from the only one who can give them to us.

The split that opens up within our very existence, between what we are and what we like to think of ourselves, grows into a self-generating cycle of illusion and alienation. For all we can see, we do not see straight. Because we do not see straight, or act straight, we end up not feeling at home, with a great sense of anxiety lurking behind all our plans and moves. For all the meaning we find in life, there remains a central crack in the picture: where is everything going and what do we really mean?

Call it a yearning to go back home, a search for integrity, a cry for forgiveness. Whatever you call it, it is an essential dynamism in our own hearts. Yet we can do nothing about it, really. We might go off on our own odyssey, searching down a thousand roads for peace and consolation, but we cannot say words satisfactory enough for ourselves, nor can we think thoughts soothing enough for our lives. We need the word of another. We need the word of God.

We need the word of one who has given us life, purpose, destiny, of the one from whom we have turned aside in our very quest for self-security. We need to have things restored.

This is a deeper level of grace, undeserved forgiveness from God who wipes away the past as much as pasts can be wiped away, who counts our past illusions as nothing and uses our past mistakes for good. (At least one man has thought that God's power consists in bringing good from evil.)

Undeserved forgiveness. Alienated from God and from ourselves, stuck in a chosen realm of dependent independence, plunging headlong from a flight too high and too ambitious, we deserve to reap exactly the ashes that come. Yet in the silence, a word is spoken. In the frenzy, a movement of peace. In the solitude, an offer of friendship.

"You were dead because of your sins and offenses, as you gave allegiance to the present age and to the prince of the air, that spirit who is even now at work among the rebellious. All of us were once of their company; we lived at the level of the flesh, following every whim and fancy, and so by nature deserved God's wrath like the rest.

"But God is rich in mercy; because of his great love for us he brought us to life with Christ when we were dead in sin. By this favor you were saved. . . . I repeat, it is owing to his favor that salvation is yours through faith. This is not your own doing; it is God's gift; neither is it a reward for anything you have accomplished, so let no one pride himself on it" (Eph. 2:1-9).

Just as we cannot grasp the real "giftedness" of our existence until we feel the frailty of our existence, so we cannot grasp the total generosity of God's mercy until we know the intrinsic alienation and rebellion sown deep in our lives. Without God's mercy, there is nothing. For this reason, we can do nothing to earn it, manipulate it, or charm it. As with creation, restoration is pure grace.

But restoration only goes so far. We already noticed that a return to "Adam's state" is only a return to the possibility of beginning alienation all over again. Along with restoration, we have radical need for re-creation. To be given, that is, new powers and principles to bring us renewal from the inside out. This is why restoration and forgiveness remain basically negative aspects of the mystery of grace; more is needed than the absence of alienation.

"If anyone is in Christ, he is a new creation. The old order has passed away; now all is new" (2 Cor. 5:17). The crucial thing that matters in human existence is that one be created anew (Cf. Gal. 6:15). The central thing that matters is that new powers and forms be given to us by which we can escape the cyclic inversion and strangulation of trying to be what we are not.

What does this newness consist of? What is the element of re-creation? Nothing less than sharing in God's very life through Christ. The ultimate meaning of grace is that mankind shares in a real way in the life of God. God's ultimate generosity lies not merely in making us, not merely in restoring us, but precisely in giving us himself.

"That divine power of his (of Christ) has freely bestowed on us everything necessary for a life of genuine piety, through knowledge of him who called us by his own glory and power. By virtue of them he has bestowed on us the great and precious things he promised, so that through these you who have fled a world corrupted by lust might become sharers of the divine nature" (2 Pet. 1:4-5).

To share in the divine nature—in powers beyond those of our nature—is the essence of grace. It is abiding in God, and God abiding in us (1 John 4:16; John 15:5). It is so sharing in the person of Christ, and the glory of God radiates in and through us. So Paul cries out that Christ lives in him (Gal. 2:20). His Spirit dwells in us (Eph. 2:22). As Jesus himself shares the Father's life, so his followers share his life (John 6:57). The intense unity between body and spirit in human nature mirrors the unity of Christ to his body, and, therefore, to the members of his body (1 Cor. 12:27).

Here the scope of the transformative work of Jesus Christ becomes manifest. Here the point of salvation, the object of the sacraments, the mystical sensitivity of Christian life, become clear. As each zipper strand is made to latch into its matching strand, so the drives of human nature for fulfillment, for love and eternal life, for peace and penetrating wisdom, for something more that we can immediately see and piece together, find their complement in the invitation from God to share his very life.

To be accepted by God in forgiveness finds its necessary counterpart in being made acceptable for God. When God accepts us, he changes us. Otherwise, salvation would simply be another way of looking at human nature as it is. Here we would be, the same old people, locked into failure, but now merely *considered* a success by God. This simply does not work. This robs God of his full transcendent power. For when God accepts us in his mercy, his power must reach down into the labyrinth of our spirits, healing, renewing, making acceptable, working in and through our life to change it so it may become, in reality, a success—an achievement because God is achieving in us.

And God's achievement in us is really that—something he works in us which would be totally beyond our comprehension and ability were not God working. No one can demand God's forgiveness. Neither can anyone share in God's nature at will. God invites. God forgives. God renews. God opens up his life to us.

*

With all God does for us in grace, how can we fail? With the full force of his love directed at us, how can we escape change and transformation? Because the human spirit always can turn in on itself. God works through the freedom he has given us so that we open up as he opens himself up, so that we turn to him as he turns to us. Since we cannot do this on our own, we have the need for God's grace. When God's grace is given, then we can turn. But even if that grace is given, we can still refuse to turn, finding the shell of salvation in ourselves, fragile and empty. Salvation is up to God, but it is also up to us.

Yet this is no place for stinginess. God is generous with life and grace; God's work is *his* work. No one can dare to restrict, predict, or interdict the grace of God. His grace remains the internal and saving work of his transcendent power. To trap it is impossible; to manipulate it is blasphemy. For this reason, the Church, aware of its own graced existence, does not consider itself the parameter of grace. If God works in and through the Church, choosing and sanctifying, he also continues his divine power working outside the Church. Jesus, after all, has been made Lord. The point of his life is to bring salvation to all. As Lord, Christ's purpose cannot be frustrated by culture or historical circumstance.

No one, then, can declare God's grace to be absent in a particular life or situation—not if he is a follower of Christ. Though we must constantly call ourselves and others to deeper levels of living in God's life, we do not have the task of damning or denouncing simply because God has been explicit with us and implicit in the lives of others. God is capable of great subtlety. His followers, in Christ, are called to be the same.

*

We are not alone. We have wanted to be at times. We have sought to insulate ourselves, figuring that if anyone knew the answer, we did. We have underestimated our helplessness. We have overestimated our despair. Yet we have not been alone.

Intimate, encompassing, persistent, subtle, God has still wanted us, sought for us, begged for us. God has been seducing us through the blatant lives of his prophets, the hidden inferences of his scriptures, the direct appeal of his Son, the secret tugs of our own lives. We have worked with the pieces for generations; we still have the puzzle. We have bandaided and dallied with a thousand quick solutions. We have tried everything but returning, opening our hands and receiving, opening our hearts and living.

We have ended up in our alleys, crying in the night, beaten, attacked, desperate. God has heard. God has given. God has come down the alley to meet us, lift up our heads, carry us to healing and friendship. He has joined himself to us so we may be one with each other and with him, one with life, one with light.

Grace means we have not been neglected. Grace means God is on our side, in our hearts. Grace means transformation has taken hold. Why is there something rather than nothing? Why doesn't our life come apart at the seams? Why have we been chosen and blessed out of all the specks in universal space? Why else? Because God is here.

10 Faith

Even the best of friends do not understand each other always. At least some of my friends will all of a sudden say, "I don't understand you;" and, thinking back, I must admit it's difficult to understand some of them, too.

We know a person's moods, facial expressions, talents, vocabulary, interests, ideas. We have long association with them, hours of conversation, trips taken together, projects, plans, golf. Yet we keep waiting, watching for the moment when an attitude or word will expose a hidden core, an inner mainspring, that explains the personality of someone. We do not understand him. We cannot unearth his secret motivation, his unsuspected fears, his personal vision.

Occasionally we get a glimpse. A friend will confess he's afraid. Another will undertake a seemingly hopeless project for the sheer joy of it. Someone will go forward where we would sit back. Someone will say the perfect thing at the perfect time.

Even so, when we are moving right to the center, we do not understand. Indeed, we hardly understand ourselves. For all our introspection and psychological zip, we do the craziest things with such bluntness that we even startle ourselves. Bursting with laughter out of the blue; a surprisingly vindictive statement to an innocent question.

Perhaps the greatest danger to modern life is the political acquaintance we are forced to have of each other. We do not even attempt to discover someone's heart. We assess, instead, their strengths and weaknesses, categorizing, summarizing, trying to muster useful knowledge so that we know what we can get and what is beyond our reach. We do not take the time to know someone from the inside, to feel what they feel. It has gotten so bad that we hardly take the time to know ourselves from the inside, getting out of joint with our feelings, with our deepest hopes.

But we don't give up, really. No matter how much another remains a mystery, no matter how much we remain mysteries ourselves, for all our ingrained manipulations, we seek the inner core. Our friends are important. They show us goodness in many forms. They bring a joy in just being themselves. So we find ourselves believing.

We find ourselves trusting in others, placing in them secrets that were bursting inside, discovering in them compassion and help. We find ourselves stretching our understanding so that we can fit them into it, expanding our minds so that we grow more like another, sensing without having to speak, intuiting without having to search.

We leap. We go beyond ourselves into another's world that, for all its ordinariness, strikes us as unique, penetrating, bursting with new facets and feelings. We leap beyond ourselves by an almost mystic insight, finding that someone's eyes can give sight to our own, another's mind can bring vision, another's heart can show what love means.

Friendship is only one form of mind-leaping that enhances our lives. In so many ways, we are the product of someone else's life, a revolutionary's dream, a scientist's searching, a poet's singing, a person's praying. Without these leaps, life would be so flat that it would stop from sheer narrowness.

*

The leap of understanding is an unsuspected thing. No one decides he is going to have an insight. With a suddenness and swiftness, the insight emerges. Not a product of will, not inevitable, not even from luck, the insight lunges forth when a problem has been pushed from every direction and there seems no other way to go. If one stumbles on an insight, usually desperation is the cause.

Thus, Copernicus made the sun the center. Kant found meaning in our minds rather than meaning simply "lying out there" for the mind to grasp. Marx made economics basic. Freud constructed the libido. And Einstein decided that light and light alone is a constant and invariable.

These revolutions in human thinking have changed the outlines of our very consciousness and even changed the face of the world. Once the insight is attained, everything bends under its sway. The earth is not absolute, the mind of man is. Revolutions must emerge to expunge exploitation. Man exploits himself by his very drives. Space and time are not normative; speed slows clocks, and mass approaches infinity as it approaches the speed of light.

Much as these insights have altered the fabric of our consciousness, they do not affect us as much as personal insights in our own lives. For each of us has our own absolute, our own values, our own sense of life and meaning. Struggling with problems that beset our lives, we go from insight to insight, attempting to wrench ourselves from the absurd.

The attempt is usually successful. For we cannot long endure absurdity. Unless some meaning is etched in our lives, things break down. We cannot do our jobs, plan our lives, fall in love, make decisions, survive. Whether in tiny bits or in broad sweeps, we are forced to tell a story about ourselves that indicates who we are, where we are going, and what we expect from life.

Our story progresses as we progress. At the age of ten, we hardly have any story to tell. But at the age of twenty, things start falling into place. We talk of studies, of a job, of someone we love, of family plans. Still later, at forty, we have a different story to tell, born of different problems. Have we been a success? Is our life secure? Do we look backwards to what we have done, or can we see something ahead for us to do? When we have reached eighty, our story is about finished. It is then a story of achievement or of failure, of goals attained or missed, of personalities formed or malformed.

The story we are making of our life is as crucial or more crucial then even the insights of human geniuses, who shape the general consciousness of man. For we can personally get by without penetrating the fabric of the universe; but we can hardly make it without penetrating the fabric of our lives. At some point, we simply must decide about ourselves, whether we are lovable or not, whether fools or not, what our values are, what we are willing to live and die for.

So we enter the tunnel. A dark, deep tunnel whose end is not readily in sight. We make a story whose end we do not know; we go on a journey without any clear destination. For at some points, all the sense we have made so far will crumble. It will not be adequate, nor satisfying. New experiences, new pressures, new bits of information will force the seams we have sewn to come apart. A moment of crisis. The tunnel indeed is dark.

Inside the tunnel, everything is scrambled. Our presuppositions, attitudes, hopes, fears—the whole way we make sense out of life goes into suspension. Somehow more sense must be made. Somehow we must see more profoundly, more widely. We need a handle on existence and, search as we may, we do not know if we'll find one. So we sift, wander, grope, scratch.

And then comes some light. We cannot explain it. We have not deduced it. But a stunning suddenness takes hold of us and we are, surprisingly, at the end of the tunnel. We have come to deeper insight, a deeper vantage-point on life, and everything starts falling into place with ease. We retrace our steps but cannot find out exactly how we arrived at the end of the tunnel, how insight was attained. There are elements that cannot be explained, connections that were mysteriously joined, steps taken without even realizing it.

As existence itself emerges as a gift in our development, so the coming to insight or wisdom emerges as a gift as well. To suddenly see. To have light where there was none. To attain wisdom. To find satisfaction. Somehow, beyond our choice, beyond our control, insight comes to claim us.

*

Christians call faith the deepest insight into life. Faith is the choice to see everything in terms of God. Faith is the absolute that all men instinctively face, an absolute that stares us in the face when we dare to look

—or are forced to look.

Faith comes about when viewpoints fail. Perhaps they fail outright, perhaps they simply fade away. Perhaps they are wrenched from us. But at one time or another there comes the choice of making ourselves divine or finding divinity (what is most important, most demanding, most fulfilling, most assuring) in someone else. For a while, we try ourselves: our minds, our satisfactions, our desire for power. When we have fallen on our faces, we give up that attempt. Then we try another person: we find the love of our life, and make that person divine. No one seems more beautiful, more insightful, more consoling, more engrossing. But love itself sees that another person is just that, another person like myself, who cannot play God.

Is it all, then, a hoax? Have we nothing to look forward to than seventy years of attempting, pretending, grasping, achieving—with all the slippage and disappointment that inevitably comes? Are we merely atoms in the void, a joke spawned by coincidence, the merriment of matter? If we are true to ourselves, we must say "no." It will not wash. This is the tunnel. This is the odyssey of every man.

Faith is the end of this tunnel. Faith is the gift that says we cannot trust ultimately in ourselves, nor explain ourselves, nor make our own meaning. Faith looks to Someone who can look on us in love, who can offer purpose and meaning, who makes the joke into a venture that we can take seriously.

Faith is the gift by which we come to assess ourselves and our world in terms of God himself. Because faith deals with God, it affords the deepest and widest viewpoint. Recognizing life as the product of a loving and transcendent God opens up vistas which no mind dares to construct on its own. The Being behind all being, the Answer behind every question, the Direction of every act, the Depth behind every surface, the Wisdom behind all knowing: God, transcendent Lord and loving Father, deals with me so I may deal with him.

Dealing with God seems like a preposterous idea: that we, fragile puffs of reality, might have contact—and intimate contact—with One who is reality himself seems bold, overconfident, pretentious. And, indeed, it would be that, were it not for the realization that faith itself comes from God and is his way of transforming our knowing so we can know in and through him.

If God is to dwell in us (which is what we mean by grace in its full sense), then there must be a change in us. The change in our knowing is called faith. When our mind comes in contact—personally, deeply, effectively—with God, then faith is present. Here the insight is pure gift, the gift of sharing in God's own knowledge, as we share in his own being.

Peter stood at Caesarea Phillipi when Jesus asked what people thought of him. Peter could have said many things, accurate descriptions of how Jesus appeared to the crowds. But instead Peter says, "You are the Messiah, the Son of the living God." And Jesus immediately points out that something is going on here that Peter cannot explain by himself; a truth has taken over which affects all truth. "Blest are you Simon, son of John. No mere man has revealed this to you, but my heavenly Father" (Matt. 16:13-16). Peter sees because he has received the gift of seeing. He sees not the surface, not the color of Jesus' eyes or hair, but he sees who Christ really is. And this vision is not attributable to Peter. Although Peter witnessed many of the words and actions of Christ, although he must have pondered what really was going on with this Galilean who entered his life, Peter's witnessing and pondering remain precisely that: openings and searchings. It is God who brought Peter's searchings to an end, who filled the open mind of Peter with the essential insight about Christ, which eluded so many others and which came to full fruit with Peter only at a later time.

As we cannot grasp our total existence, so we cannot grasp the ultimate scope of our life. We are basically receivers of everything we have—and receivers of faith as well. For this reason, faith cannot be forced on anyone. One who cannot see simply cannot see. Artificial vision will not suffice.

But real vision *does* suffice. Faith performs an extensively transforming work in our life. The gift of God's vision dominates the whole framework of our thought. All of us have absolutes, even if we change those absolutes every day. Behind everything we do, there is an object that makes sense to us; when the object is great enough, we find sense in our whole life. Faith makes sense out of our whole life and our whole existence. We understand ourselves as personally in contact with the One who is most real; we understand that Someone to be a loving Father who cares for us, who is personally involved in us. We begin to see patterns in our lives which form a dialogue between God and us, his pursuing us and our pursuing him, even when we think we are fleeing. The logic of the Son becoming our brother brings home the intense fellowship that God wants with us. It also graphically points out how much we are worth in God's eyes. The outpouring of the Spirit charges all our thoughts and actions so that we become different people, people who live in breakthrough.

To see as God sees, in whatever way we can, brings about a revamping of our values. It *is* utterly crucial whether God seems like an arbitrary tyrant or a loving Father. Once I am convinced about what God is like, my view of reality itself changes. Illusions that were harbored, fears that were hidden, hopes that were suppressed can be dealt with in a new light.

Yet, personal as faith is, it must also be communal. The personal dimension of faith means that God is not only known and affirmed; it means that he is loved with the total energy of our hearts. The communal dimension of faith means that this God, in whose wisdom I have been permitted to share, also shares his wisdom with others. Our faith is a *shared* experience. Faith cannot be an esoteric form of knowing or a private philosophy constructed out of desperation. Rather, it is a public acknowledgment of what God has done which profoundly brings the awareness of God into our minds and dramatically brings us into the heart of God. If faith were an esoteric form of knowing, or a purely private philosophy, then the God in whom we had faith would be a private God or an irrelevant God—in other words, he would be no God at all. For this reason, faith must be public. The God of belief has created the only world there is, has addressed himself to the whole of mankind, and has given himself for the salvation of the world.

*

If faith perfects our capacity to understand, then there is no need to view faith as the failure of human reasoning. Often it seems that faith demands the renunciation of reason and intelligence. Like sacrifices paid to a deity, we pass in our common sense and accept the insane as sane, the black as white.

Really, intelligence has little to do with it. Whether our I.Q. is 160 or only 80, the drive for faith would be the same. Perhaps we might grasp the need more sharply, perhaps we might articulate more precisely; yet even the most intelligent of men can understand the tremors of his existence and not think his way through them. Intelligence brings us a better understanding of the problem but not of the answer. That is to say, no genius of his own intellectual strength can bring an answer to his life.

For we are dealing with the passion of the human heart, the surge to go beyond itself in order to find itself. Because the heart must expand beyond itself, it cannot give itself faith. Only God's power, beyond ours, can do that. But going beyond itself is an act of love, of choice, and not the conclusion to a syllogism or the balancing of an equation. So the sense that faith makes has a total satisfaction about it. What is deepest in our hearts is responding to what is deepest in existence. We can choose not to respond. But we ultimately do not respond with our minds. We respond with our whole selves.

Because we respond with our whole selves, our intelligence is included in the response. In faith, nothing is lost. We do not set our minds aside, nor the values of our lives aside, nor our own selves aside. Instead, in the thrust of faith, we find our intelligence, we find our values, we find ourselves. What is set aside is the illusion that misfocuses our sight, the nondiscretion that distorts our values, the alienation that tears ourselves apart.

So St. Paul talks of the folly of human wisdom,

but his object is not to leave us wisdomless. Far from it. "There is, to be sure, a certain wisdom which we express among the spiritually mature. . . . What we utter is God's wisdom" (1 Cor. 2:6-7). It is a wisdom that does not destroy our wisdom so much as it takes it over and allows it to peer into places that seemed impossibly dark. It is a wisdom that takes what *seems* to be so, disciplines it, and brings us what *is* so. Rather than a flight from reality, faith brings us face to face with reality.

If faith seems strange, this is because it allows our search for the true and the real to surge as it did not seem possible. And yet, there is nothing impossible about faith. As we know through other people, expanding our knowledge through their wisdom, so we can know through God, bringing our knowledge to the absolute and most expansive wisdom. That we have not worked this knowledge out completely on our own does not mean it is any less our knowledge; it simply means that the comprehensive knowledge of faith must be grown into, that the ranges of belief must be wandered through and probed before we know the "breadth and length and height and depth of Christ's love, and experience this love which surpasses all knowledge, so that you may attain to the fullness of God himself" (Eph. 3:18-19).

Faith makes us feel small, but so does life itself, when we really see it. The smallness faith brings is the only way we can come to the vastness faith offers, as the paradox of reality would have it. To reject the possibility of faith, however, means that we are adequate to ourselves, that we have all the answers or can easily find them, that the limit of our minds does not include anything beyond our minds, that we are, in fact, divine enough as we are. If these positions seem absurd, then we have moved close to seeing the marvelous brilliance of believing, the magnificence of God and man in touch.

*

We have all reached, at some time, the edges of our lives. We have pushed and pushed until we are at the wall. Things could not be more frightening, more unsettling, more depressing. Yet we have gone on. We believed. We put our life in perspective. We saw something greater than our life holding it, sustaining it, giving it some kind of guarantee.

We really have no choice in belief. It is part of the fabric of every life. So fragile do we seem, so mysterious, such an unexplainable appearance in the universe, that we turn to something else to give that life its basis. If we turn to ourselves, we turn to an expanded picture of ourselves, projecting onto ourselves a role greater than we have. If we turn to another, a fellow stranger, we find a friend, someone we can trust, but not someone who ends the search, really, for a friend actually joins us in the journey.

So there it is—the chance for faith in God. Why not? He is waiting and we have nothing to lose.

11 Love

We hate to be trapped. We have our handy collection of exit lines just in case we are: I've got an appointment. I wish we could talk more, maybe some other time. Gee, you got me on my busiest day.

We want the ability to dart and dash according to our whim, sailing free and easy, attaching and un-attaching without any strings. Boy, do we hate strings. Strings that hold us back, strangle us, keep us from moving on, fix us in one spot. We want to live our lives like some mythical cyclist buzzing over never-ending dunes on the Pacific.

So why are we always caught? Is it some innate bashfulness that ties us where we don't want to be? Or some future promotion? An angle that we're working that will pay off at a later date? Sometimes benefits like these make it worthwhile for us to put up with restrictions. Pay now, get later.

But sometimes we're in even deeper than this. Sometimes we just get stung far more violently than we figured. We talk into a web whose filaments not only contain us with devastating effectiveness: worse, we love the entanglement, we love being caught, we never want to get loose.

In other words, sometimes we fall in love. The free and easy style goes by the board as we gravitate inesbapably toward the one we love, panting, preying, putting out everything we have just for the company. Here we are, committed bachelors and spinsters, mocked by the magnetism in our own hearts, a fool for love anyhow. We may regret it at times, longing for the good old days of uncommitted bliss. But we are sold, trapped, tied helplessly down—and for the most part we like it.

It would be a waste of words to try explaining this phenomenon. All of us have gone through the transition in one form or another. Few of us freely chose the move: we were, literally, caught. Cupid stalked us, aimed the arrow, and down we went in unconscious confusion. There is nothing to explain, except to note the phenomenon, modestly commenting that no one can really escape it, that those most convinced of their immunity to love end up sometimes stung the hardest.

*

There is no great difficulty in discovering what love means if we think of the automatic love people expend on themselves. Not necessarily when they are staring in the mirror, or talking about themselves, or taking off an afternoon to pamper themselves. Even more, the instinctive way we do almost everything for our own good reveals the scope of our self-love. We view the world as a field to gratify ourselves. From rising in the morning, through any busy day of eating, working, riding, thinking, to the last semi-thoughts at night, everything is considered to be for myself, my pleasure or my advancement. In short, I am the center. We love what is at the center of our attention, our energies, our lives. First off, that means we love ourselves.

The crisis of love consists when the trap is sprung

and we are forced to expand that center to include another beside ourselves. In fact, no chore is more difficult. For the constant temptation is to revert back to a cryptic form of self-love instead of really loving another. We are attracted; we get caught up in the difficulty of loving the attraction, the pleasure, as much or more than we love someone else. Someone turns me on. Someone is striking. I enjoy another's company. Sure enough, I end up loving the experience of being turned on, of being struck, of having company. And I run the risk of missing the person on the other side.

At times it seems hopeless, that all love really is self-love, that love is quite impossible. Or does love demand that we go on a renunciation binge, severing every passion and attraction, until our love reaches some ethereal level of being pure and disinterested?

Not if we can tell the difference between a feeling and a choice. For love is a matter of choosing in its mature state. Consider: that we rarely have *feelings* about ourselves; our narcissism takes a subtler course. We simply choose the things that seem to benefit us. Occasionally there may be feeling, but choice is what makes for love.

So we solve the crisis of love when we learn to choose in terms of another as we choose in terms of ourselves. Once we have placed another at the center of our lives, whatever feelings are involved in this, then we are in the position of truly loving another, beyond mirage, beyond self-interest.

This seems to be the point of Jesus' reply when asked about the greatest commandment. He replies, "The Lord our God is Lord alone! Therefore, you shall love the Lord your God with all your heart, with all your soul, with all your mind, and with all your strength.

This is the second (commandment), You shall love your neighbor as yourself" (Mark 12:20). Jesus is talking about centers. If we center our life around someone, then that someone is loved the same as we love ourselves. Center, Jesus says, your life around God and your neighbor, just as you center it around yourself.

For isn't it obvious that we love ourselves with all our heart, mind, soul and strength? We have a practical form of idolatry going on most of the time, an idolatry built into our very systems. The only solution for one who idols himself is learning to idol another. Jesus states that the one we must idol is God. When we have learned to act in terms of God, then we have found love and also a way to get beyond ourselves to others.

No wonder we have to be trapped into love. Getting beyond ourselves seems an impossible task. The flimsiness of our own existence makes us tend to accumulate, grasp, manipulate, pout. It takes a while to learn to go beyond ourselves; it takes a long while before we learn how to do this well. We can be easily trapped into love; but we can spend a lifetime learning to love as we should.

In fact, we hardly know how to love ourselves well. For gratifying ourselves does not mean we are loving ourselves. Our spirits spin off in so many different directions that good often ends up circumventing good. We respond to what is near at hand and destroy the long range good, mistaking lust for love, greed for justice, violence for accord. Like a child, we grasp with instinctive vigor for bits of candy, bypassing true nourishment. Why is it so hard to know our true good and true evil? Because everything, to someone or other, looks good at some time. Why is it so hard to do good, to really love? Because with a reverse Midas-touch we often turn good into evil because the total picture escapes us.

When we lie, cheat, kill, fornicate, reject worship, renounce faith, collapse under pressure, live by hatred, we are reaching for what seems good. This is how we are ordering things about ourselves. But what seems good is not good, for we have clutched at the nearest straw, considering it a log. We have not looked at our whole life and its meaning. Our eyes are turned in, only toward ourselves.

It is so easy to be deceived in love. We get trapped, but not trapped enough. We think that something is done out of love, but it ends up being backwards love, or hate. We imagine that training can conquer the problem—rules, therapies, philosophies, moralities are constructed as a guide to true love, to the good. We are so deluded that we think if we know what is right, we will do what is right. Hardly. For we can all catalogue times when we knowingly and fully took a course that spelled simple hate—and we did it out of perverse love for ourselves.

*

"This is how all will know you for my disciples: your love for one another" (John 13:35). Perhaps if we truly learned to love ourselves, to do what was for our own good, we might be able to love another well. Perhaps if we learned to center things on ourselves properly, we might discover how to center things on another. But even this is hard to learn. So untrusting are we, that we leave deep fingermarks from clutching too hard. We clutch too hard at things because we are afraid to let go, afraid to trust, afraid, even, to know

ourselves. For all we love ourselves, we doubt our own
worth.

We think if we could only provide our own worth,
make our own security, know the full scope and meaning of our life, then love would be easier. At least we
would not play our cards so closely; we might take a
risk or two, plunge into the deep, know what is right
and do it because we had nothing to lose.

But we are too fragile. Every time we secure our
own security, it falls apart. Jesus classically shows this
in the parable of the rich man who accumulates a vast
amount so he can say to himself, "You have blessings
in reserve for years to come. Relax! Eat heartily, drink
well. Enjoy yourself." But that very night he loses his
life (Luke 12:16-21). Our desire to be financially secure,
or sexually secure, or politically secure, or emotionally
secure—secure in any way—falls apart under the ultimate insecurity of our existence.

If we can love only when secure, and our security
cannot come from ourselves, where can it come from?
It can only come from God. Yet, if we are so untrusting, or caught up in ourselves, how can we trust God? If
we could place our trust in him, then perhaps we can go
beyond ourselves for once, then perhaps we could find
out how to love. But how can that be?

God must act first. He must ground in us the very
trust we place in him. He must reach through us, so
that we may reach out for him. The only solution to
our seemingly insoluble anxiety lies in the recognition
of God's deep love and care for us. When we have seen
that existence is not hostile, fate not cruel, life not
blind, then we can move out. But to be able to see this
means someone does care, God does care.

Yet God's care is not hidden in obscure mental

twists or fantastic strokes of luck; it is present all around us, in the very generosity of our being, in the insight that all is freely given to us. But we have become so insecure that we take the very gifts of creation for granted. We use them as occasions of grudging and hedging. (I got mine, baby; you get yours!) The possibility of security is obscured. The knowledge of God's love is lost in the casualness of our life.

So God breaks apart the casualness of life through his direct revelation in Jesus Christ. Jesus, God's grace and wisdom, is also God's love. In the directness of Jesus' life, man sees God directly: caring, curing, giving, trusting. "God's love was revealed in our midst in this way: he sent his only Son to the world that we might have life through him" (1 John 4:9).

And when our insecurity mounts to such fury that the showing of God's love itself in Jesus generates hatred and insecurity, generates the murder of Christ, God's love still shines forth. No more graphic image of love has evolved than the image of Jesus, the God dying for those who hate him. This death, which reveals so starkly our own weakness, reveals as starkly the almost naive enthusiasm of God's love for us.

It also reveals the ultimate possibility of trust. Trusting in God in the face of death, the collapse of life, the extinction of consciousness, the pain of being pushed to the very edge: this shows the real meaning of trust, the meaning of Jesus' trust. And the resurrection of Jesus was the vindication of his trust. "It was thus that he humbled himself, obediently accepting even death, death on the cross. Because of this, God highly exalted him" (Phil. 2:8-9). This Christ who trusted brings the results of trust: the power of God to resurrect, not only his Christ, but all who trust in him.

This power, then, is the basis of Christian life. It is nothing else than sharing in Christ's life itself. We, who are baptized in Christ, partake in his death and his resurrection (Romans 6:3-5). This power brings to us, stamps on our very persons, the love of God. "Love, then, consists in this: not that we have loved God, but that he has loved us and has sent his Son as an offering for our sins" (1 John 4:10). The whole internal model of our existence is transformed from one of grasping to one of reaching out, from mistrust to confident trust, from anxiety to peace.

For who can doubt his worth before God, when we have been saved "not by any diminishable sum of silver or gold, but by Christ's blood beyond all price" (1 Pet. 1:18)? We are worth the price of God as dramatically as he can reveal that price. What, then, is there to fear? How can I stay inside myself, defining everything in terms of myself, making myself the norm, when I know I have nothing to lose for all is mine in God? To the insecure Corinthians, applying labels and creating rivalries, Paul writes, "All things are yours, whether it be Paul, or Apollo, or Cephas, or the world, or life, or death, or the present, or the future: all these are yours, and you are Christ's, and Christ is God's" (1 Cor. 3:22-23).

In Christ, then, we have the possibility of trusting in God because we know of God's love for us. With the possibility of trust, we have also the possibility of love. The insecurity knotted to our frame is severed by the blade of love. Not only, though, *can* we love; we have as well a *model* of love, Jesus Christ. "This is my commandment: love one another as I have loved you" (John 15:12). And not only have we a model of love, we also have the *power* to love, through the very Christ living within us. "There was a time when you were dakness, but now you are light in the Lord. Well, then, live as children of light" (Eph. 5:8).

For God's love of us consists in placing us at the center of his being. We are inserted into God and loved as God loves himself, empowered as God is empowered, cherished as he cherishes himself. For when the Son becomes man and sends forth the Spirit on man, in Christ man is lifted into the very structure of God, loved as the Son is loved, sealed with the Spirit as God's being is sealed by his Spirit. As love indicates a free exchange, a mutual presence, and open intimacy, so the Christian, who receives God's Spirit in Christ, is called "friend" and "son" of God (Cf. John, 15:15; I John 3:1; Gal. 4:5).

The dynamic of trusting under the power of Christ so we might be empowered to love stretches itself out as a whole way of life for the Christian. Having the possibility, the model, and the power to love, the Christian can do nothing else than love—love truly in God. For anything else is contradictory. Anything else is simply not being what we are. The essence of Christian life, then, is being what we are.

As a way of life, a way of *living*, Christianity surpasses any ethic or philosophy. The test for ethics rested with the law. The law expressed God's will for us—what God saw as best for us. This was a necessary thing inasmuch as we have such a difficult time knowing what is really best. But law, as such, only made clearer the obligations flowing from our being. It only increased the pressure on us. Insofar as we were inadequate to that pressure, the law was viewed as oppression.

The empowering love of God frees man from the

oppression of law because the inadequacy of man is transformed through the presence of Christ's Spirit in us. "The law was powerless because of its weakening by the flesh. Then God sent his Son in the likeness of sinful flesh as a sin offering, thereby condemning sin in the flesh, so that the just demands of the law might be fulfilled in us who live, not according to the flesh, but according to the spirit. . . . But you are not in the flesh; you are in the spirit, since the Spirit of God dwells in you" (Rom. 8:3-9).

How else can St. John conclude that the Christian, as a Christian, does not sin (1 John 3:6)? He is merely concluding from the internal logic of what it means to *be* a Christian, to be transformed into a new state of existence in Christ. The logic is inescapable. "No one begotten of God acts sinfully because he remains of God's stock; he cannot sin because he is begotten of God" (1 John 3:9). To love is to love as God loves; not to love is to be outside of God. To die with Christ means we are dead to sin; sin has no place in the Christian's life (Romans 6:7).

Yet, look at us Christians. Sinners to a man. Reborn in Christ, the old genetic makeup keeps re-occurring. Again, a return to selfishness, to insecure anxiety, to the drive to manipulate, destroy, defy. Once again, we are plunged into the heart of evil, the mystery of existence. Are we merely repeating in Christian terms what was the problem in human terms? Are we transferring problems and escaping any solution?

To think that we have only transferred the problem would distort the whole view of the Christian life. The presence of evil in the Christian life cannot be smoothed over by anything less than the expectation of its total elimination. To say that evil in human action will remain, but that it makes no difference, or is not really evil, or is forgiven beforehand, or any other cover-up, would take the power of Christ and render it null and void.

So, it may seem, the presence of sin destroys the power of Christ. If he were truly powerful, we would not sin. We would live perfectly transformed lives. But such a tack shows a certain unfamiliarity with human life and the work of God.

The power of Christ is abundantly clear in the lives of those who do attain to love. While no one bats 100 percent, batting gradually becomes better under the sway of Christ's Spirit. The point to see is that the principle, the root, of love has begun to take hold. The growth is sometimes slow, because we are slow to recognize the dullness of our hearts. Like the transition from sickness to health, however, there comes a breaking point where the antibodies finally get a hold on the disease-causing organisms. This is why the same John who insists that the Christian does not sin can at the same time insist that acknowledgment of sin is necessary (1 John 1:8). At one point John is looking at the seed come to full flower, at another point he is looking at the seed as it begins to sprout, still embedded in the dirt.

Freed from the "law," empowered with love in order to love, the Christian must embrace openly the power that Christ pours into him through his dynamic Spirit. We should expect nothing automatic about this, however. We should expect a gradual growth into fullness as we learn more deeply what it means to live in Christ (Cf. Eph. 4:11-16).

For this reason, Christianity is a combination of high expectation and gentle patience. Expectations there must be, or else we are merely looking at human nature in another way. If we do not expect to achieve a solution to the human dilemma, then we have no business in religion. Religion is not to coat a bitter pill. Religion is to deal with people as they are and bring people to where they should be; where, in their hearts, they know they must be. Yet such a passing, from where we are to where we know we must be, consists of slow and delicate transitions arched out over years of meditation, examination, confession, and renewal. No transition of any sort can take place without Christ's power. But once a battle is won in a certain area, then the extension of victory grows with increasing proportion. Christ achieves his glory in us (Phil. 2:13). His glory is achieved according to our nature, with a view to its final fulfillment.

Is there any place for a "law" or "ethic" in Christianity? Of course, but its place is a finely hewn niche. Laws, as such, along with advice and theories, can do nothing for our behavior. Once the power to change and love acts, only then can laws help mold the shape of the change. But Christian laws are basically insights from the model of Christ himself, implications from the very meaning of what it means to be a Christian.

If Christ's whole life, summed up in his death and resurrection, is worship, a Christian cannot have a blasé attitude toward worship. If God has saved us as a community, no Christian can scorn the community of believers. If our worth has been established by God, then we cannot undercut our worth with acts of partial or complete self-destruction (and even too much television can be partially suicidal). If God has appeared in our bodies, then treating bodies as evil, cheap, mere commodities, is inconsistent. When Christ reveals the truth of God, what business have we with lies? If ultimate evil is expressed in the killing of Christ, then what kind of killing can a Christian tolerate? If marriage expresses the very covenant of God with his people in Christ, how can Christians renege on a promise made in and through Christ? If God forgives so lavishly, can hearts be joined to him and still be hard and unforgiving? If God creates and redeems with such utter generosity, who can live in God and be cheap, stingy, unwilling to share what he has?

The law of Christianity is the law of our own hearts, transformed in Christ. That we do not know our own good is clear enough; that God has shown us our own good when he came down "for us men and for our salvation," as the ancient Creed says, clarifies our vision. That the good we know often is not done seems obvious; that Christ enables us to do the good we see in him is called grace.

*

If it makes sense to see love as the basket that holds all the eggs, then we have a Catholic mind. If it makes sense that the twisting of love's dynamism has often left man stranded, then we share a Catholic view of the problem. If it makes further sense to view God as loving, as giving himself to us, as indwelling and transforming our actions and wills, then we uphold Catholic dogma. If it finally makes sense to have man pursue a life of love through gradual change and renewal, to live up to high expectations with wise compassion, to gradually become perfected in Christ, then we partake in a Catholic attitude.

If love, however, seems impossible and illusory; if

it seems insignificant; if God appears to be always distant, placing ridiculous goals on us to chase for success; if we expect instant holiness, on the one hand, or a constant "winking" at human follies, on the other hand, then we have the very difficult task of telling the human heart it is an illusion, or wiping the very meaning it has sought from the human spirit.

The surging of the human heart beyond itself can be stunted in many ways. But the ultimate dynamism, the sheer force of our need to love, either must be satisfied or else causes breakdown. Love demands ecstasy, standing outside ourselves—this is what the root meaning of "ecstasy" indicates—in another. God has stood outside himself within us. His doing this affords us the chance for our deepest security and most profound consolation. Precisely because of this, we can dare to survey our life, to acknowledge our needs, to expand ourselves with the same generosity of God. We can do this because the love of God, Christ himself, has been poured into our hearts through his Spirit.

As with faith, there is little choice. We must believe in something; so too, we must love something. We can escape the trap only so long. We either get outside ourselves or stay locked in them forever, believing that the range of our sight is the range of everything. The latter alternative has been viewed as a kind of death, a living death. For are we not dead when we have no place to go?

12 Living

Let's look at traps again: not the trapping done between the sexes, as effective as it is; not even the trapping done by one person to another. All of us have felt caught, as if between the floor in an elevator, without even an emergency button to push: trapped by our families, our jobs, our routines.

Rather, I want to talk about the trapping we do inside ourselves: internal, home-made traps—for example, the self-image trap. I think that I must be devastatinglingly intelligent, or helplessly handsome, or sparklingly witty, ever strong, ever smiling—or whatever other image I get fixed on. Then the trap starts to close with no exit in sight: I cannot live up to my expectation. I am inadequate to my image, at odds with my image. But, still, I will not yield. I continue, instead, to suffer.

Or, take the judgment trap. Somehow, in the hazy days of our weaning, we got the impression we were tolerable, but barely so. Somewhere in our past, strange words were pronounced over us; "We've got to put up with you, much as we hate it. We have no choice." Somehow, we feel judgment was passed on us and we spend the rest of our lives executing the sentence. Inferior. Not up to par. Guilty. A runt. And, sure enough, whenever the chance occurs, we carry out the sentence by undercutting our position, devaluing our strong points, making ourselves fail, trying to win the wall-flower prize of the century.

Or, take the competition trap. What makes Sammy run can be anything, so long as it makes him run. Eying others, I make life a game in which winning is secondary to the urge to win, a gasping affair before the final ecstasy of ulcers or heart attack. Style, grace, pizzazz, push, pull: all roads seem to go up, so it makes no difference what road I take. Like the jerking but successful flight of the fly, I buzz in squarish circles.

People-traps. My traps. A way of life—but not a way of living.

*

Living seems to encompass so much that everything said about it could be platitude. Living is war; living is also little girls blowing on flowers. So what else is new? We have Pepsi commercials to teach us about living: enough is enough!

But living is different from life. Life floats like a cloud, just there, formless, able to assume any shape wanted. Life can mean simply *having life*, the passive reception of a gift that enables me to stare intelligently out into space, drift from place to place, without purpose. Life can simply mean *being alive*, the passive state of minimal alertness, minimal activity, minimal me. Life can be a ho-hum affair.

Living, however, is life in movement. Rather than the passive reception of a gift, or the passive retention of a state, living involves the active engagement of myself. The formless takes on form. The potential becomes actual. Through my choosing, acting, considering, risking, I find direction—I give my life direction.

To give my life direction does not simply mean having a goal. How many goals have we pursued, only to set them aside through fatigue or miscalculation? Some goals are real, others illusory. Maturing as a person and as a Christian entails sifting through the range of goals chosen or shoved upon us, disciplining the bunch, making some goals real and discarding the rest.

Having a goal only begins the process of giving direction to my life. The following step is equally important: allowing that goal to shape my life so that everything comes into focus at certain points. As children learn to direct the flow of water from hydrants on the city streets in summer, we learn to direct the flow of activity, thought, and event in our lives.

Maybe we can imagine what living means; maybe we are already truly living. If so, in either case we've realized what busting self-traps is like. For we can only be trapped by ourselves when we have no direction in life. Our nerves wiggle with weakness when we don't know where we're going. Our life seems valueless when it seems to add up to nothing. We judge and condemn ourselves because we see nothing to justify ourselves—in fact, when we look at our lives, we see nothing at all, only a puff of smoke, only a tortured mannequin, only an insignificant toy. We probably go trapping ourselves in order to redeem ourselves. We figure if we sink ourselves enough, if we end up dazed in our own personal skid row, then we'll somehow force ourselves to find direction; we'll force ourselves to swim or drown.

Busting open the traps of life demands the critical but natural art of pinning down goals, taking stock, assessing strengths and weaknesses, eliminating the unsettling bulk, and targeting the flow of life in the chosen direction.

When we've done this, we know something of free-dom. We know enough of freedom to make life an expression of our innermost selves. We have learned that *living* makes life into a statement, an affirmation of myself, an expression of who and what I am, a vi-brant masterpiece of existence.

*

The parameters of Christian life that we have dis-cussed (Church teaching, Church action, faith, love) can become traps as well. Too many have fallen into the dizzying world of dogma, expending more on the force or cleverness of expression than on what was to be expressed. Many as well have found the sacred sac-raments to be excellent magical analogues: a swish of water, a bite of bread and, presto, the illusion of instant salvation. Faith easily becomes the excruciating search for a so-called certainty of salvation. Likewise, we all know those who have woven the cords of faith into whips with which they beat themselves hourly, daily, yearly. Even love, the seemingly unshatterable power, can be twisted into self-hate, the glorifying joy of eating mud.

Trapping ourselves with religion arises from in-complete conversion, flinching transformation. Not that God withdraws the transforming power of his life and being; rather, we close off the door to God, revert-ing to those instinctive human reflexes that God's power seeks to change. We lose track of our goals, we get diverted, we make our Christian lives ambiguous expressions, attempting to collapse ourselves from with-in through residual cynicism.

Church teaching and action are supposed to be

forms of living; faith and love should likewise be structures of living. So the time involved in gradual transformation really amounts to the time spent by Christian people in learning how to live at a deeper level, how to reorganize and refine the process of living in terms of God's words and actions in our lives. For it takes no little discipline to grab our lives by the shoulders and make them do what we want them to; similarly, it takes no little work to allow God to grab us directly and infuse our spirits with his mighty but subtle power.

The grace of God makes living possible and viable; letting God's grace do what it must brings the process of transformed living to completeness. So when Jesus says that he has come that we may have life, and have it more abundantly (John 10:10), he obviously isn't talking about life in the flat, formless sense—having more of that would be absurd! He's talking about a level of living, an engagement of the components of life into a field of full and fulfilling living. If we settle for less than this, we have short-circuited the program of salvation itself.

When we mature enough to do Christian living, we make our lives a prayer. Just as true living consists in the intense expression of what and who we are, so true Christian living consists in the expression of what and who we are in Christ. "Live on in me, as I do in you," says Christ (John 15:4). Make the transforming action of God ring through every part of your life until you are a living parable of God's reign.

For the goal of the Christian is nothing else than God's reign, his kingdom. This is what Christ lived for, what he came to bring. His parables, his actions, even his denunciations, were all at the service of this kingdom. Indeed, at the point of his death, he still shares the kingdom with a thief good enough to know even a thief needs it: "Lord, remember me when you come upon your reign" (Luke 23:42).

We could be victimized by the illusion that the kingdom of God is a totally future thing, a goal that exists as a reward for avoiding certain obstacles, for doing prescribed works. Illusions die hard. Perhaps, then, here is the underlying motive for preserving Jesus' statement on the kingdom: "You cannot tell by careful watching when the reign of God will come. Neither is it a matter of reporting that it is 'here' or 'there.' The reign of God is already in your midst" (Luke 17:20-21). Seeking the kingdom exclusively in the future or exclusively "up above" both contain the risk of missing the kingdom altogether.

Unless the kingdom comes about in our present lives, it cannot come at all. Unless it is a goal both abiding within and stretching beyond our present lives, it simply is not the kingdom. Unless pursuing the kingdom becomes a daily way of living, we have renounced what it means to be a follower of Christ.

Can there be any other meaning behind Jesus' parables depicting the gradual growth of the kingdom —the mustard seed, the leaven (Matt. 13:31-33)? Why else paint the kingdom in the ambiguous figures of weeds and wheat growing together if not to portray the ambiguity of the kingdom emerging in our ambiguous lives (Matt. 13:24ff.)? Isn't this the real logic of sending works out explicitly to proclaim the coming of the kingdom (Luke 10:1-20, esp. 9)? The kingdom begins *now*!

So the Christian aims for the kingdom. The kingdom of God encompasses his whole life and gives it direction. Serving the kingdom and bringing it to fullness creates the movement of authentic Christian living, a

wordless prayer don in a language in which we ourselves are the signs.

*

If living itself becomes a prayer, it is done in
various modes. To express the full range of living
prayer would be impossible. At the risk of burlesquing
this richness, I simply want to dwell on two states of
prayer, listening and responding.

Listening

When our prayer listens, we stand in intense
alertness to a God speaking to us, wrapping us in his
word. This is a mode of contemplation, of reception,
but not a mode of inactivity and suppression. For everything we are is received; to pray by listening is to
become more what we are. We let the flow of life become a refreshing stream before it goes surging back
over the rocks and crevices of our existence. The water
is the same, the living is the same, the prayer is the
same: it simply exists in a stiller state.

Intensity characterizes this prayer; concentration
gives it substance. From many directions, threads,
hints, clues, we discover meanings and messages. Samuel's simple words, "Speak, Lord, your servant is listening" (1 Sam. 3:10), show the stance of listening
prayer: my ears are raised, my eyes opened, nothing
gets my attention except the word of God. For God's
reign demands a relationship with him, a union in him,
analogous to Christ's union with the Father. Christ
finds his very life in the Father (John 6:57), his good

doing the will of his Father (John 4:34), his life an intense listening to the Father (Cf. John 5:19).

Yet Christ was no petty or narrow listener. He hears the words of his Father in himself (he is the word!), in the scriptures which take on new scope in his wisdom, in the diverse people—fishermen, lawyers, the workingman, the poor, the sinner—whom he meets, in the everyday events of life, in all of nature. His gaze takes everything in and sanctifies it—dedicates it to God, sets it aside for the kingdom, makes it part of his living.

Christ the listener shows listening as an aspect of lived transformation. His ability to pursue a goal gave direction not only to his life; it still gives direction to the lives of millions of his followers. He is himself, then, the model of listening prayer for the Christian.

Our scope of prayer should be as extensive as his. For we, too, can concentrate our attention on the God dwelling within us, on the Spirit of Christ guiding our life, on the abundant gifts of this Spirit who awakens in us the mind to see everything in terms of God; on ourselves, our families and friends, even on those who misunderstand us; on the events that we encounter, the decisions we have to make, even the mistakes that end up helpful; on the small things of daily life, on the great things of nature. All can be part of God's kingdom, his reign of grace and glory, slowly growing to its fullness.

Listening prayer constitutes an essential dimension of the Church's living. God's word comes with stark and powerful force during the readings at worship. The community faces its roots, the narration of God's deeds in history—not as a nostalgia binge, but as a contemplative pointer to God's present deeds in our very own history. God's word breaks apart the worn and trivial patterns of life to demand that we truly live; our ideas must stretch, our hearts must search, our actions must expand; we must be stunned with wonder.

God's word drives men and women to spend their entire lives contemplating it. It drives scholars to exegete it, preachers to explain it, reforms to spring from it. It gives the community of Christ the nerve to continue when doom is forecast, the peace to pace itself through events of every sort, the strength to maintain its conviction in doubt, the urge to question in complacent times.

The words of the liturgy flow through seasons of the year and seasons of life, attuning us to hope, joy, penance, trust, faith, fulfillment. Architecture and art represent a more profound bending of the elements of life: for we ourselves are molded, heated, pounded, carved, embellished, reshaped through the force of God's speaking to us. The vision that results is a fearless one: we receive eyes to view the entire universe without flinching, the entire span of life without dread. For all is part of God's speech, all part of his vocabulary, all aspects of the syntax of his love whether nuanced, whether direct.

To neglect this prayer of listening is to play with death, for listening constitutes a basic point in the cycle of our living. A Catholic who does not listen is not a Catholic at heart. Rather, he has decided all the answers are ready given, prepackaged, obvious, at his fingertips, his disposal, his mercy. So whole sections of his life are severed from God's word, and the brunt of God's word is severed from his living. As a result, a nonlistening, nonpraying Catholic does not really live. He's a puppet, gestures without a soul, movement without a spirit. When he reflects upon his life and God's word, he does so with a mirror that does not capture anything beyond surface glimpses; to truly reflect, we need a retina to catch all, living nerves to transport it, a brain to encode it, a heart to accept it and make it our own.

Responding

Listening prayer, even though it is crucial, is only part of prayer. Prayer must also act in another way; it must respond.

Whenever energy is received, it must expend itself in some direction. When the energy of God's word is received through the range of Christian living, it must expend itself through the directions of a changed life. A changed life expresses itself through changed actions. As we know who and what we are, we are forced, through internal persuasion, to express this in what we do.

This is living prayer, for it makes all of living into a response to God's word. We become, in fact, words of God, his love and dedication incarnate in our deeds, our lives statements of his goodness. Our deeds express not only ourselves, but ourselves enlivened by God—God's own life running through us.

Responding prayer branches out, in a general way, into the vocations of Christian living. Each is called; each responds. Most respond in a way demanding dee-pest sacrifice and self-giving: marriage. Loving another does not receive its challenge at any particular state of time so much as through the totality of time. I love not just in my youth, not just in my prime, in my success or difficulty; I love completely, with all my time, my achievements, limitations, energy. And this is done in the prayer-filled sanctification of daily life through marriage. For what life is as daily as married life? Yet what life has such powers to sweep so much into the reign of God? Married partners express in themselves the love of God for all men, the dedication of Christ for his Church. In all they do, Christ acts: sustaining, supporting, enriching, nourishing, begetting, educating, suffering, rejoicing.

Married men and women reflect the love of God throughout time; but some are called to reflect the timeless love of God which they do through sacramental orders and religious life. Here the riches of marriage are set aside not from fear, nor from puritanical instincts. Instead, the demands of God's kingdom come with such a force and urgency that marriage does not fit in. Men and women called to this vocation expend the energy reserved for marriage directly on the Church, in its teaching, preaching, worship, care for the sick, the elderly, the poor, the oppressed. Such a radical state of life, though, is no more radical than Christ's own. In one way or another, it has always been with the Church; it will always be.

The single person who is not a priest or religious also carries on a vocation. Whether openly chosen or the product of circumstance, the single state can be a vehicle of outstanding Christian living, for here men and women have the time and resources to expend themselves in a diversity of situations which life opens up to them. Individuals needing help, the needs of the parish of local church, special projects, unnoticed services—the opportunities are endless and the call to respond all the more pressing. What could be an occasion of selfishness can become, under God's word, the occasion of tremendous generosity.

Through these general vocations, Christians learn the real responding that Christianity entails. Whether married or single, whether religious or lay, we come face to face with the starkest human sufferings: needs, injustices, morally offensive situations, corruption, the absence of warmth, the twisting of minds, the blocking of human communication. Can the Christian stand by so many situation calling for his help with eyes turned down, away, or up? Can the Christian keep to himself, locked into some private ecstasy, when God calls so directly to him? Can life be a prayer without responding?

In no way. The love of God is given to us to be given away. The expansion of God's life through us imposes the demand that our lives expand to include the suffering as a personal concern for each of us. The more we listen, the more we are aware of what is asked. The scene of judgment in Matthew's Gospel makes it undeniably clear that to pass by the suffering is to pass by Christ in his suffering (Cf. Matt. 25).

Once again, the liturgy of the Church mirrors this state of prayer. As listening prayer is reflected in the liturgy of the word, so responding prayer is reflected in the liturgy of the eucharist. The Christian community turns to God in the very dedication of Jesus Christ, in his very self-sacrifice. The bread and wine collected together represents our lives. We acknowledge that, through God's goodness, we present bread and wine as a product both of the earth and our human work. In the eucharistic prayer, the bread is transformed into the body of Christ: "This is my body which is given up for you." The wine is transformed into his blood: "This is the cup of my blood. . . . It will be shed for you and all men . . ."

In the liturgy, then, Christ's body becomes ours; his blood runs in us. His dedication and self-sacrifice becomes the living strength for our own dedication to God and our fellow man. The transformation of the liturgy cannot be restricted only to the bread and wine; it must also be applied to us, in our movement of life, in our service to the kingdom. To respond in Christ is to have full Christian response; he makes us part of his lived prayer to the Father.

Responding prayer gives rise to the famous commitments of Christians to the sick, the homeless, the poor. It makes social reform not just a nice hobby but an inescapable task. It puts the Christian at odds with injustice and war, with tyranny and oppression. It brands every Christian as a utopian, a citizen of a greater state in which men live with each other in honesty and decency, in which all have a place, all have resources of life, in which God is served in each other, for he is all in all (1 Cor. 15:28).

*

As we have different styles of life, we may have different styles of prayer. Some may be at home only paging through the Scriptures, others in the steady reflection on daily life, some in basic prayers made into life-meditations, still others in the thrilling manifestations of God's Spirit.

But for all of us, prayer is care. Praying is caring for God's word surrounding our life at every point, for God's people calling to us in many ways—for God's kingdom that sets up a new relationship between us and him, between man and man. God cannot be careless. Because of what he has done in us, we cannot be careless either. Our lives, precious gifts from him, cannot be thrown aside or left sloppy: they must be made into living statements of the mystery of God in which we have been wrapped.

When our life becomes a prayer, we witness what transformation means, not as passive witnesses observing a curious phenomenon, but as engaged participants, becoming ourselves examples and images of God's transforming grace. We are Christ's body, alert and healthy; we are his followers, believing and loving. The peace and fullness such a life brings fills in the answer to one of the instinctive questions of our nature: What is life all about? If we would find the answer, we must begin living in depth and not be content with only the surface. If we would find the answer to life, we must find life in the living God whose kingdom is coming to birth.

13 Transformed

Growing up in a big Eastern city has made me paranoid. I'm sure I'm not unique. Every house has its dark secret, every street its potential mugger, every purchase has a hidden hook, every ride in the subway its danger, and every apartment its cockroaches.

I suppose the cockroaches get to me more than anything else because of their utter dedication and resistance to destruction. I've been places where months of diligent spraying and powdering did nothing but make *me* sick: the roaches kept right on coming, crawling through the supposedly poisonous powder, sneering at the latest potent spray.

Naturally, then, apartment dwellers are transformed into hunters: slippers, newspapers, fly-swatters, towels—anything to wipe out a roach! I've even set the alarm for a middle-of-the-night awakening so I could sneak into the kitchen, flip on the light, and smash maybe hundreds of roaches in one sadistic frenzy.

Soon they recede; they go to the next apartment, teasing a new client, testing the hunting skills of the various apartment occupants. When your defenses are down, however, they're back again, first a brave scout swimming in the sink, then a whole army eating through your walls.

The terrifying thing about the roaches is not so much their presence; we can get used to everything. Rather, the crunched bodies of killed roaches after a few minutes of clubbing disturbs any serious man. For here is spilled life, indiscriminately annihilated, dozens falling at a time, as if all there was to their existence is a few months of nightly sorties followed by the inevitable clobbering.

These moving balls of dust, hanging on from ancient times, called the most adaptable of all species, able to survive even an atomic blast—why do they bother? Are they here only to show the triviality of existence, another day, another death? For any hunter of roaches, after sweeping his victory pile together, must wonder if the roaches are not a mirror of everything, if we are only magnified images of them, born for a few quick sorties, but eminently disposable all the same.

That, my friends, is real paranoia.

*

Those of us whose environmental circumstances permit viewing the stars must get the same chill. Staring at the specks against the night, realizing that every star is at least as important as our sun, some of them are whole galaxies, and we, a tiny nothing in a huge, almost empty room. Try and think you're big against odds like that! Almost nothing. Some swirling ball whose chemicals happened to combine when lightning struck and, zap, here we are. It's enough to make you cringe.

Yet we don't. We dare to look. Rightly, we should be shamed, humiliated, cowering in the corner. Here we are, one of perhaps a billion, evidence of nature's virtuosity, but only a tiny note in an eternal symphony. Yet we dare to raise our heads, stare the stars down, and look. We do not stand in the corner. We don't

Transformed 173

count ourselves meaningless. We feel we have a place.

After all, we've dealt with huge quantities before, with one thing coming after another with endless succession. Our days have seemed endless: again and again, the same schedule, the same monotony. We have dragged ourselves through these. And we have found some meaning in every day of one sort or another and meaning in all our days combined.

We have faced generations, generations coming, generations going. Every twenty years or so a new breed comes along, demanding its care and attention; the older breed fades back and back, until the grave. But we have not stopped. We keep producing new generations. And we find some meaning in each generation, if only to criticize the new against the old, or vice versa.

We have studied history in which empires have arisen on one page and fallen a few pages later. One kingdom munches, another is eaten. Each reaches as far as it can. Each eventually overreaches. Each declines. But we have not stopped forming empires; they continue to come. Each has its unique emphasis; each yields something to the next.

By all normal reckoning, we should properly be collapsing when faced with so much revolving endlessness. By rights, we should be stunned into shock at the utter triviality and effervescence of existence. But we are not. Faced with one thing after another, like one infestation of roaches after another, we should be giving up. But we don't. Everything still maintains its importance: our nations, our generation, our day. If that importance ever left, perhaps we would give up. There would be no motivation, no spirit, no fight, no zip.

Yet it is hard to see where that sense of importance comes from. For we seem to be as disposable as anything else. We seem like quantities, numbers, statistics. We have our individual endings, but the race seems to go endlessly on. Somehow, though, we resist being just quantities. We know when we deal only with numbers, the finer things seem like extravagant waste; finer things, like our personalities. If we were just numbers, then we might just as well be machines. In fact, it would be hard to tell the difference.

Perhaps this is why death is so threatening to us. It makes us into quantities. One comes, one goes. Like the GM assembly line, everything looks different but everything is really the same. Jane Doe and John Doe, each taking up so much space, eating so much food, spending so much money. Bits of economy, bits of ecology, begetting just enough to fill the vacancy.

Here we are, facing the temptation of cynicism again, wondering if we are what we seem to be. The experience of achievement, however, strongly attacks the temptation. Achievement brings home to us a feeling of success. The strands of existence come together. Our expended energy amounts to something. Our predictions pay off. Luck has smiled on us. After wishing and working, advancing and retreating, we arrive at a breakthrough. Achievement! Victory! In a moment, which appears timeless, the past and present blend together in a stunning recognition that we have accomplished something, that something is different because we are were here. Who can say we are dispensable, our world is senseless, our work futile, our life illusory? We have done something, we have become something.

We all have experiences of achievement. Holes in one or a hard-earned par. The brilliant move at the bridge table which brings the contract home. The crafty intuition that swings a business deal. The plodding which produces the winning report. Years of labor which pay off in a diploma or a new house, the burst of applause which crowns a strenuous race. The gnawing thrill at having mastered a difficult problem and found a solution.

Man the achiever. And only he knows. Only man knows that he makes a difference.

But even achievement fades. The taste of success can be sidetracked because it is short-lived. People may applaud us, but applause dies down. Esteem fades. The thrill vanishes. Then come doubts about what we have really accomplished. Even when the achievement does not depend on the recognition of others, even when it is an independent, personal accomplishment, there is a bitter edge. It is so difficult to keep up an achievement, a state of consciousness, a level of existence. What we have become, we can un-become. The reality slips by, or drips away. All who face the crisis of aging face the effervescence of achievement. All who acknowledge the fact that they will die recognize that the noblest of paragraphs ends with some period or other.

Achievement is a victim of the time in which life itself is lived, a time that includes beginnings and endings. And while achievement wrenches us from the endlessness of monotony, it cannot wrench us from the grasp of time, unless that achievement passes beyond time itself, beyond beginnings and endings. Achievement, if it is to truly satisfy, must sum up our whole lives, at a point that includes birth and death, at a point that transcends birth and death.

For all our attempts to pin a timeless, trans-temporal level of existence to ourselves, we, of ourselves, cannot bring ourselves beyond time. We cannot "prove" our immortality with the certainty that we need. And even if we could, we cannot control the quality of that immortality. For to imagine existence in a dark place, blessed forgetfulness, merging with some universal ideal, even an eternal quest for truth, by no means automatically spells achievement. Instead, it could all be endless frustration.

Surely, the instinct of immortality cannot be easily brushed aside. The transcendent dimension of man remains precious, potent, pointing to a timeless existence. How, after all, can we ask and answer so many questions, each projecting forth to another, each opening up to what still lies ahead, and believe that we were meant to stop that questioning, to cut the very process short? How can we experience the drive to love with unrestricted fullness, to give ourselves more and more, and think that such a drive should shoot only so far and then suddenly stop. The mystery hints of more. But only in Christ does that mystery take shape.

*

This is why the Resurrection of Jesus is so decisive from a Christian's viewpoint. Here achievement really means achievement. It is a timeless breakthrough in which a whole life, in all its dimensions, in all its time, surges together at a level of existence that spells triumph. Speculate as we might about an immortal life, there remains no certitude about such speculation until we confront the image of the risen Christ. Here possibility becomes actuality, vague thoughts become concrete being, hopes become achievement.

Christ's resurrection stands as the ultimate elevation of life beyond its dimensions. The writer of the apocalyptic book of Revelation places on the lips of Christ these words: "I am the Alpha and the Omega, the Beginning and the End" (Rev. 21:6; 22:13). And in the Catholic Easter liturgy, begun in the darkness of night, after the Easter candle is lit with newly struck fire, the priest intones, while scratching the present year into the candle: "Christ yesterday and today, the beginning and the end, Alpha and Omega; all time belongs to him and all the ages; to him be glory and power, through every age and forever. Amen."

The achievement of Christ is not, then, merely being raised to the level of existence he manifested during his short ministry; rather, Christ is shown at the fullest level of existence. He is the Lord, sharing the transcendent power of God as his own. And this achievement is what Christ promises to his followers. Mankind achieves in him. "Whoever wins the victory shall inherit these gifts; I will be his God and he will be my son" (Rev. 21:7). This can happen because the Christian, through the worship and life of the Church, has died and risen with Christ. "Since you have been raised up in the company with Christ, set your heart on what pertains to higher realms where Christ is seated at God's right hand . . . After all, you have died! Your life is hidden now with Christ in God. When Christ our life appears, then you shall appear with him in glory" (Col. 3:1-3).

So the achievement that shatters the triviality of existence belongs to Christ, who brings together in himself the beginning and end of all existence, who focuses the fullness of life in the risen glory of his state. That achievement extends as well to all who share the life of Christ, through the grace-filled presence of Christ in every faithful follower. All that matters, then, as far as our achievement is concerned, is whether we share in the risen life of Christ or whether we do not. This is the demarcating line of existence. If Christ lives in us, then we have every expectation of sharing his glory. For Christ has conquered death (1 Cor. 15:54-55).

*

The widespread expectation of the end of the world prevalent among the early Christians undoubtedly arose from the experience of Jesus' resurrection itself, perhaps aggravated by apocalyptic ideas associated with the destruction of Jerusalem (Cf. 1 Thess. 5:1-4; 2 Thess. 1:9; Luke 21:5-24; Mark 13:5-31; Matt. 24:1-35). But interest in the end of the world, while remaining intense, subsided into a gentle agnosticism. "As to the exact day or hour, no one knows it, neither the angels in heaven nor even the Son, but only the Father" (Mark 13:32).

As enthusiasm for the world's end became more subdued, the early followers of Jesus were able to reflect in less stark terms about human destiny. Paul undergoes the most development. He writes to assure the Thessalonians that the dead will have an equal share in the resurrection of Christ. They feared that only the living would be entering the kingdom when Christ comes. "We would have you be clear about those who sleep in death, brothers; otherwise, you might yield to grief, like those who have no hope. For if we believe that Jesus died and rose, God will bring forth with him from the dead those also who have fallen asleep believing in him" (1 Thess. 4:13-14). In this way, the living have no advantage over the dead.

This expands further into an idea of the Lord's rule over both the living and the dead. "While we live we are responsible to the Lord, and when we die we die as his servants. Both in life and in death we are the Lord's" (Rom. 14:8). The presence of all, whether living or dead, to God, finds beautiful echo in Jesus' put-down of the Sadducees, who refused any idea of resurrection. "As to the fact that the dead are raised, have you not read what God said to you. 'I am the God of Abraham, the God of Isaac, the God of Jacob'? He is the God of the living, not of the dead" (Matt. 22:31-32).

We may not seem endurable, but the word of God, the life of God, is (Cf. 1 Pet. 1:23-25). And if that word of God is given to us, can we ever be without it? If God's power and life extends to all, whether living or dead, can the dead be seen as nonexistent? Christian reflection said no. The dead exist in God. Here the dramatically revealing stories of Jesus raising the dead must have had their impact on the early Christian believers (Cf. Matt. 10:18-26; Luke 7:11-17). The raising of Lazarus in John's Gospel (John 11) couples by association with Jesus' parable about Lazarus and the rich man. His parable, in fact, shows a real existence after death, even before the full restoration of the world (Luke 17:19-31).

God's power over the dead and the living leads to a recognition of existence for the dead; all who die in Christ live. Paul himself, who pushed so strongly in his desire for the end of the world, recognizes the peace of dying before the final fulfillment. "I long to be freed from this life and be with Christ," Paul writes (Phil. 1:23). That being with the Lord permitted no separation from him (Cf. Rom. 8:35-39) formed an essential breakthrough in Christian understanding. The risen Christ exercises his Lordship irrespective of our views of time, of life, of death. This alone afforded witnesses to the Gospel, the incentive to yield life itself, since death had been emasculated.

Through this development, Christians came to see endurance in Christ as a double-decker stage. The first stage dealt with our immediate existence after death, irrespective of the human body. In this stage, achievement or frustration are experienced to the extent of our existence which is not yet complete. When the second stage comes, when creation is fulfilled on the "Last Day," then achievement or frustration will be fully experienced, for then the whole of creation, in every dimension, physical and nonphysical, will be completed.

We understand each of the levels in this double-decker view the same way. At each level, achievement, grounded in Christ, is projected from the experience of achievement in this life; failure, as the absence of achievement, is likewise projected from the experience of failure in this life. The state we have before God in this life, then, structures the state we will have before him in completion. What will fully come receives its trajectory from our life in time.

This is another way of saying that the kingdom of God has already begun. The fullness we expect in Christ begins in this life, with our experience of Christ in community and grace. Achievement is only the extension of this Christian life; failure is merely the extension of the absence of this Christian life.

We can understand the achievement which we call heaven as the intensification and stabilization of the good we have grasped in this life. All the love, peace, joy, generosity, fellowship, sacrifice, and richness that comes from life in God are stabilized and intensified in our state of achievement. Our sharing in Christ's wisdom, our communion with him and others, our living in his love, flower into unseriected life with him.

We can similarly understand the failure that we call hell as the intensification and stabilization of the absence of good we brought about in this life. The hate, envy, overreaching, frustration, pride, and personal poverty that come from our rejection of God remain with us. Blindness, loneliness, myopic self-love, shrivel into the horror of a person who knows no joy because he cannot get beyond himself.

Belief in heaven and hell runs a great risk, for we are often tempted to bring these final stages into our present life. While heaven and hell flow from this life, we cannot presume to project the final state of anyone from how they appear to be living. We do not have the task of judging (Matt. 7:1-2). Too often Christians have drawn circles around the "chosen" and painted everyone else as reprobate and damned.

Once we are perceptive enough to admit the existence of nuanced gray states between the so-called "white" of innocence and "black" of guilt, then we have to admit as well some pressure release between heaven and hell to allow for the ambiguous in human life. The idea of purgatory is such a release. It prevents our projecting achievement or failure too readily into human life. It acknowledges that, good as we may be, there tends to remain some residual selfishness and insecurity. It proposes that all, before the attainment of heaven, who are not totally enlivened in God's life, who are not fully transformed, will undergo further transformation and perfection before full achievement in God is experienced.

Hints in the New Testament of purification beyond death (cf. Matt. 12:32; 1 Cor. 3:14-15) must also be re-enforced by scriptural sentiments of care for the dead if our fellowship with the dead is to make sense. The apocryphal book of Maccabees speaks eloquently of prayer for the dead (2 Mac. 12:43-46), and the canonical epistle to the Corinthians notes the primitive custom of vicariously baptizing those who have died (1 Cor. 15:29). A Christian mentality that wrenches itself from contact with the dead shrivels. The lines of Christian community perdure in God. Thus, those who live in the achievement of heaven can assist those preparing for heaven. And those struggling to live their life in God can assist those still being transformed in death.

Perhaps we cannot know too much about heaven, hell, and purgatory. Until we experience these dimensions ourselves, they must remain projections of our experience of the risen Jesus. But these can be eliminated only with the greatest risk. To eliminate heaven is to restrict God's power and deny the fullness of Christ's life to his followers. To eliminate hell is to deny our ability to renounce God and make choices that affect the ultimate meaning of our lives. And to eliminate purgatory (as some kind of transformation for the imperfect) is to ignore any nuance in moral and Christian life.

*

If we cannot know much of heaven, hell, and purgatory in the middle stage between death and creations' fulfillment, it seems we can be even less certain of what the final fulfillment will be like. For while we can deal with concepts of peace and love, failure and frustration, we are stunned in our attempt to imagine the physical dimension of human fullness. Our minds play with the images of Jesus after his resurrection, showing his wounds, eating fish to prove he wasn't a ghost, passing through doors, appearing in different forms. Here is our only view of total human fulfillment, and we are stumped.

What is going on here? What can possibly be in store for us? How, we wonder, will all these people be raised from the dead? Where will they live? Will the world be the same kind of place as it is now? Will we be wandering from planet to planet, future planetary charioteers? Will we be young or old? If we are maimed, will we be restored? The questions are endless.

Our only approach to these questions lies in probing the meaning of human fulfillment in our imaginations, stretching to a dimension that pushes our experiences of time and space beyond ordinary boundaries. Here it helps to dream a little, letting poetry and science fiction run together. Here it helps to keep our eyes firmly locked onto the risen Christ and realize the relativity of all we know. Size (vastness and smallness), time (dragging by or hurrying by or standing still), and feelings (intense, cool, idling) must all be divested of the common association we make of them from this life. Here is pure novelty, an unknown dimension, a vision of the new heaven and new earth (Rev. 21:1ff.) that bends every idea we have, that forces us to throw aside our normal measuring rods.

We do know this, however: the experience of fulfillment will contain both communal and physical aspects, for these are basic traits of our human nature. The communal dimension of fulfillment is called the "heavenly Jerusalem," a society in which men live in such contact with God that the whole framework of relating to other men is changed. The love that God gives us in grace explodes into the most intense and extreme practice: openness, appreciation, care, joy, partnership—the very feelings we have with "that someone special" in this life will extend to all because God will be all in all, run through all, filling all, glorifying all (1 Cor. 15:28). At this point, the revelation of the Church will be complete; the presence of Christ to his people will be so direct and immediate that the only metaphors the Bible can muster are those of sunlight (Rev. 21:23) and consciousness (Cor. 13:12; cf. 1 John 3:2).

The physical dimension of fulfillment means that matter will be subjected enough to spirit and meaning that it will reveal transparently and directly our personalities and the goodness of God. Our bodies, which hinder us to such a severe degree now, also reveal us. Fulfillment projects that the hindering of the body will be stifled, that what we are will shine through immediately. The goodness that God has attained in us will shape and renew our bodies so they respond fully to our goodness and, in that way, respond fully to the will of God.

*

Perhaps it is all like yeast. Slowly growing, slowly evolving, goodness gradually being added to goodness, tranformation igniting further transformation, so quietly and so subtly that we cannot realize it or point to it. Suddenly the dough is removed from the dark; its growth is revealed, full, finished, ready to be made into the richest bread.

Perhaps the alarm is set, the tic and toc taking place with a secret goal; the second hand swishing by seems a repetition, returning to the same place again and again, but really it is moving forward to the time of awakening, the crash of success, the ring of fullness, the revelation of glory's morning.

Perhaps the meaning of fulfillment and the meaning of Catholicism can have no better clue than the cry of the Visionary: "I also saw the new Jerusalem, the holy city, coming down out of heaven from God, beautiful as a bride prepared to meet her husband. I heard a loud voice from the throne cry out: 'This is God's dwelling among men. He shall dwell with them and they shall be his people and he shall be their God who is always with them. He shall wipe every tear from their eyes, and there shall be no more pain, for the former world has passed away' " (Rev. 21:2-4).

If we have any desire to pass away, not into nothingness but into transformed life, and if we feel that passage must begin now, then the richness of Catholic meaning, which exposes human meaning itself, can be the passageway to the life we've always longed to live and God has always offered.

Epilogue

The sense of Catholicism consists in expecting fulfillment from God. What other meaning could there be to creation and to the resurrection of Jesus? An unfulfilled world means a half-resurrected Christ.

But fulfillment does not come all-of-a-sudden with the swishing of a magician's hand. Fulfillment begins and makes progress in the life that God gives us now, in the salvation that is coming about now, in the transformation that is taking over now. This transforming life of God takes over our action and decisions: we call this love. It also takes over our consciousness and outlook: we call this faith. The presence of faith and love mean that we have not been abandoned in some limbo-earth; rather, God himself is present to us. For we can be saved in no other way than through contact with God. The risen Christ brings us this vital contact.

And he does this in the Church, a Church sharing in his risen power and presence in such a way that when it acts, Jesus acts. The sacraments of the Church, its sacred actions, seize the world and ourselves and bring them into contact with the saving Christ, so that no part of our lives will be severed from him. The Church acts from a background of knowledge and teaching that is the product of God's action on human history and the human mind, so that our words and images can bring us beyond ourselves. The deeds and words of the Church form God's support for us, for we cannot stand alone, in faith or anything else. We are a community, a people, a nation made holy, a society transformed by the presence of the risen Christ and his Holy Spirit. The Church is God's way of starting the heavenly city, the fulfilled kingdom that Jesus came to bring.

The possibility of transformation for our personal deeds and knowledge, our social acts and understanding, arises from a fundamental rejection of cynicism and anti-socialism. Cynicism says we are not worth saving, that our hopes and dreams are illusory. Anti-socialism says that men cannot really live together, that we are each cowboys riding off alone into our own sunset. Cynicism begins the destruction of human meaning; anti-socialism begins the destruction of human life.

But once cynicism and anti-socialism are rejected, then we can see the brilliance of God's plan of salvation: that God actually takes his creation seriously enough to save it, to bring it to its full potential, to bring it God's own glory. God does not destroy his creation, nor cure it with halfway measures. Instead, he transforms it, destroying creation's evil, preserving its good, transforming its powers. He does this in Christ, who, becoming man, shows how valuable we are; who, dying, destroys and nullifies sin; who, rising, destroys death and bestows the transforming power of his life.

In Christ, the transcendent power of God is revealed, a power that belongs to him alone, but a power which he does not use capriciously and arbitrarily; he uses his power to heal, restore, cherish, and perfect. In Christ we see God acting in our world, becoming part of our world, saving our world.

*

This book has been written to show that Catholicism is not an arcane collection of superstition, nor an arbitrary manipulation of human thought, nor an irrelevant relic of more gullible times.

Catholicism is real, alive. It is a stunning merging of human instinct and faith, human longing and hope, human passion and love. Catholicism starts where we start, with the unavoidable parts of human nature. Its history is an assembly of human action, its thought an assortment of human wisdom. Throughout the range of human feelings and actions, God has been working; God has dared to believe in us, to risk himself on us, to blend himself with us. When God and man merge, Jesus comes on this earth. When Jesus comes, his followers follow.

Who can adequately say why they believe in anything? How can I say why I am a believing Catholic? Perhaps it's the boldness, to think that God does take us for real. Perhaps it's the diversity, this stable framework for so many people and so much human outpouring. Maybe the richness has its play: the ritual, the life of prayer, the high demands, the wise compassion.

Mostly, though, I find God acting in the Catholic Church. I find him in the worshippers on Sunday, in the simple women making visits to Church on warm afternoons, in the torturous turns of my own heart which pursues and flees God with alternating regularity, in the men and women who have found courage to continue when life dealt a bad deal, in the faces of children which open wide with the stories of Jesus, in the human dedication of its clergy and sisters, in the humility of its kneeling in prayer, bowing in adoration.

I have tried to say that Catholicism can respond to the needs of the human heart, pouring God's power into our lives. I cannot "prove" this. But I think it makes sense, the same sense that a human being makes, the same sense that God makes.

Yet Catholicism cannot be discovered by reading and thinking; it can only be discovered by praying, by letting our spirit lead us to the highest point it has ever sought, and by letting the Spirit of God, ranging the extent of our heart, reveal and caress.